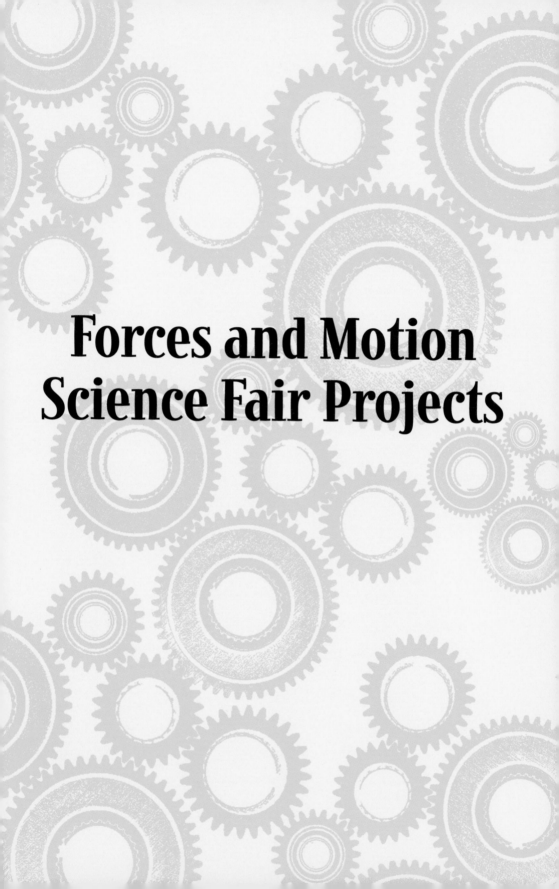

Forces and Motion
Science Fair Projects

Library of Congress Cataloging-in-Publication Data

Gardner, Robert, 1929–
 Forces and motion science fair projects, revised and expanded using the scientific method / by Robert Gardner.
    p. cm. — (Physics science projects using the scientific method)
 Summary: "Explains how to use the scientific method to conduct several physics experiments with forces and motion. Includes ideas for science fair projects"—Provided by publisher.
 Includes bibliographical references and index.
 ISBN 978-0-7660-3415-0
 1. Force and energy—Experiments—Juvenile literature. 2. Science projects—Juvenile literature. I. Title.
 QC73.4.G374 2010
 531'.6078—dc22
                        2008050066

Printed in the United States of America

092009 Lake Book Manufacturing, Inc., Melrose Park, IL

10 9 8 7 6 5 4 3 2 1

Illustration Credits: Tom LaBaff and Stephanie LaBaff

Editorial Revision: Lily Book Productions

Design: Oxygen Design

Photo Credits: Sean Nel/iStockphoto.com, p. 78; Shutterstock, pp. 3, 6, 24, 44, 98, 126.

Cover Photos: Christine Yarusi (hands); Sean Nel/iStockphoto.com (bungee jumper); Shutterstock.

Revised edition of *Forces and Motion Science Fair Projects Using Water Balloons, Pulleys, and Other Stuff.* Copyright © 2004.

Physics Science Projects
Using the Scientific Method

Forces and Motion Science Fair Projects

Revised and Expanded
Using the Scientific Method

Robert Gardner

 Enslow Publishers, Inc.
40 Industrial Road
Box 398
Berkeley Heights, NJ 07922
USA

http://www.enslow.com

Contents

Indicates activities appropriate for science fair projects.

Forces and Motion Experiments and Projects Using the Scientific Method

Physics is the part of science that deals with matter and energy. You and the world around you are made up of matter. All activity involves energy. By understanding physics you can unlock the secrets of matter and energy, from the movement of planets across the sky to the sinking of a three-pointer in a basketball game.

In this book you'll discover how forces, machines, and motion work, not by reading about the physics behind them, but by removing any mysteries through experimentation.

Much of the work physicists do involves measuring things. Therefore, you'll begin by taking some measurements and seeing how they can be used to understand the properties of matter and energy.

◄ Astronauts can conduct physics experiments to study the properties of forces and motion in weightless conditions.

Experiments and Projects

This book contains lots of fun experiments about forces and motion. You will also be given suggestions for independent investigations that you can do yourself. Most of the experiments are followed by a section called Science Project Ideas. This section contains great ideas for your own science fair projects.

Most of the materials you'll need to carry out these activities can be found in your home or school. Several of the experiments may require materials that you can buy in

a supermarket, a hobby or toy shop, or a hardware store. Some you may be able to borrow from your school's science department. Occasionally, you'll need someone to help you with an experiment. It would be best if you work with friends or **adults** who enjoy experimenting as much as you do. In that way you'll both enjoy what you are doing.

If any danger is involved in doing an experiment, it will be made known to you. In some cases, to avoid any danger to you, you'll be asked to work **with an adult**. Please do so. Don't take any chances that could lead to an injury.

Like any good scientist, you'll find it useful to record your ideas, notes, data, and anything you can conclude from your experiments in a notebook. By so doing, you can keep track of the information you gather and the conclusions you reach. Your notebook will allow you to refer to past experiments and help you do future projects.

How Scientists Search for Answers

When scientists have a question to answer, they start by researching. They read scientific literature and consult online science databases that are maintained by universities, research centers, or the government. There, they can study abstracts—summaries of reports—by scientists who have conducted experiments or have done similar research in the field.

In this way, they find out whether other scientists have examined the same question or have tried to answer it by doing an experiment. Careful research will tell what kind of experiments, if any, have been done to try to answer the question.

Scientists don't want to repeat experiments that have known and accepted outcomes. Also, they want to avoid repeating any mistakes others may have made while doing similar experiments. If no one else has done scientific work that answers their question, scientists then do further research on how best to do the experiment.

While researching for the experiment, the scientist tries to guess—or predict—the possible results. This prediction is called a hypothesis.

The scientist hopes that a well-researched and carefully planned experiment will prove the hypothesis to be true. At times, however, the results of even the best-planned experiment can be far different from what the scientist expected.

Yet even if the results indicate the hypothesis was not true, this does not mean the experiment was a failure. In fact, unexpected results can provide valuable information that leads to a different answer or to another, even better, experiment.

Using the Scientific Method in Experiments and Projects

The Scientific Method

A scientific experiment starts when someone wonders what would happen if certain conditions were set up and tested by following a specific process.

For example, if the angle at which a dart is fired from a dart gun is changed, will that change the horizontal distance the dart will fly? Some possible hypotheses might be:

✓ The dart will fly the same horizontal distance no matter at what angle it's fired.

✓ The dart will fly farther horizontally if fired at a moderate angle.

✓ The dart will fly farther horizontally if fired at a steep angle.

Let's say your hypothesis is that the dart will fly farther if the dart gun aims at a steep angle.

For a start, we have to know that a scientific experiment has only two variables—that is, only two things that can change. For this experiment, one variable would be the angle at which the gun is fired. The other would be horizontal distance the dart will travel.

Nothing else is allowed to change, not the power of the dart gun or the size of the dart, not the levelness of the ground over which you're firing. This is because if anything else

besides the two variables were
allowed to change, it wouldn't be
possible to tell what caused the
change in the distance the dart
traveled. Now, if the experiment is
carried out and no difference is observed in distance traveled,
it wouldn't mean that the experiment is a failure. Even if your
hypothesis that the dart will travel farther when fired at a
steep angle turns out to be false, all results—positive or negative—provide important information. The results can lead to
further ideas that can be explored.

In this book, you'll be conducting scientific experiments. The
results of these experiments and the conclusions you reach may
lead to new experiments that you can carry out for yourself.

Scientists may develop logical explanations for the results
of their experiments. These explanations, or theories, must be
tested by more experiments. If the resulting data from experiments provide compelling support for a theory, the theory
could be accepted by the world of science. But scientists are
careful about accepting new theories.

If any of the experimental results contradict a theory, then
the theory must be discarded, altered, or retested. That's the
scientific method.

Basic Steps in the Scientific Method

The best experiments and science projects usually follow the scientific method's basic steps:

✓ Ask questions about what would happen if certain conditions or events were set up and tested in an experiment.

✓ Do background research to investigate the subject of your question.

✓ Construct a hypothesis—an answer to your question—that you can then test and investigate with an experiment.

✓ Design and conduct an experiment to test your hypothesis.

✓ Keep records, collect data, and then analyze what you've recorded.

✓ Draw a conclusion based on the experiment and the data you've recorded.

✓ Write a report about your results.

Your Hypothesis

Many experiments and science projects begin by asking why something happens. In this book's experiment "Weightlessness on an Orbiting Satellite or Spaceship," the question is, "What causes astronauts to feel weightless in an orbiting satellite or spaceship?"

The educated guess (the hypothesis) that answers the question is, "The orbiting vehicle is actually falling constantly, dropping from under the astronaut if he or she is not held down."

How do you test this hypothesis? First you should study the nature of gravity and how satellites and space vehicles go into orbit. Some background research into how astronauts train in weightless conditions will prepare you to understand the forces and motion involved in your simple experiment.

You should find out what methods, equipment, and tools for measurement are needed to design an experiment that will test your hypothesis. By using the right tools and materials—in this case Styrofoam cups, rubber bands, a spring scale, and an elevator—you can actually observe and measure the effects of weightlessness.

Remember: To give your experiment or project every chance of success, prepare a hypothesis that is clear and brief. The simpler the hypothesis the better it is.

Designing the Experiment

Your experiment will be structured to investigate whether the hypothesis is true or false. The experiment is intended to test the hypothesis, not necessarily to prove that the hypothesis is right.

The results of a well-designed experiment are more valuable than the results of an experiment that is intentionally designed to give the answer you want. The conditions you set up in your experiment must be a fair test of your hypothesis. For example, in the dart experiment, you may have to pay attention to the force of the wind, and whether you are firing into it or with it. You also have to be sure the enlarged protractor you drew is accurately divided into degrees.

It's most important that the experiment's procedures and results are as accurate as possible. Design the experiment for observable, measurable results. And keep it simple, because the more complicated your experiment is, the more chance you have for error.

Also, if you have friends helping you with an experiment or project, make sure from the start that they'll take their tasks seriously.

Remember: Scientists around the world always use metric measurements in their experiments and projects, and so should you. Use metric liquid and dry measures and a Celsius thermometer.

Recording Data

Your hypothesis, procedure, data, and conclusions should be recorded immediately as you experiment, but don't keep it on loose scraps of paper. Record your data in a notebook or log-book—one you use just for experiments. Your notebook should be bound so that you have a permanent record. The laboratory notebook is an essential part of all academic and scientific research.

Make sure to include the date, experiment number, and a brief description of how you collected the data. Write clearly. If you have to cross something out, do it with just a single line, then rewrite the correct information. Repeat your experiment several times to be sure your results are consistent and your data are trustworthy. Don't try to interpret data as you go along. It's better first to record results accurately, then study them later.

You might even find you want to replace your experiment's original question with a new one. For example, the experiment that begins with the question, "What causes astronauts to feel weightlessness in an orbiting satellite or spaceship?" brings up another question: "What would happen if the satellite orbits against the rotation of the Earth instead of with the rotation?"

Writing the Science Fair Report

Communicate the results of your experiment by writing a clear report. Even the most successful experiment loses its value if the scientist cannot clearly tell what happened. Your report should describe how the experiment was designed and conducted and should state its precise results.

Following are the parts of a science fair report, in the order they should appear:

• The Title Page

The title of your experiment should be centered and near the top of the page. Your teacher will tell you what other information is needed, such as your name, your grade, and the name of your science teacher.

• Table of Contents

On the report's second page, list the remaining parts of the report and their page numbers.

• Abstract

Give a brief overview of your experiment. In just a few sentences, tell the purpose of the experiment, what you did, and what you found out. Always write in plain, clear language.

• Introduction

State your hypothesis and explain how you came up with it. Discuss your experiment's main question and how your research led to the hypothesis. Tell what you hoped to achieve when you started the experiment.

• Experiment and Data

This is a detailed step-by-step explanation of how you organized and carried out the experiment. Explain what methods you followed and what materials and equipment you used.

State when the experiment was done (the date and perhaps the time of day) and under what conditions (in a laboratory, outside on a windy day, in cold or warm weather, etc.). Tell who was involved and what part they played in the experiment. Include clearly labeled graphs and tables of data from the experiment as well as any photographs or drawings that help illustrate your work. Anyone who reads your report should be able to repeat the experiment just the way you did it. (Repeating an experiment is a good way to test whether the original results were obtained correctly.)

• Discussion

Explain your results and conclusions, perhaps comparing them with published scientific data you first read about in your research. Consider how the experiment's results relate to your hypothesis. Ask yourself: Do my results support or contradict my hypothesis? Then analyze the answer.

Would you do anything differently if you did this experiment again? State what you've learned as a result of the experiment.

Analyze how your tools and equipment did their tasks, and how well you and others used those tools. If you think the experiment could be done better if designed another way or if you have another hypothesis that might be tested, then include this in your discussion.

• Conclusion

Make a brief summary of your experiment's results. Include only information and data already stated in the report, and be sure not to bring in any new information.

• Acknowledgments

Give credit to everyone who helped you with the experiment. State the names of these individuals and briefly explain who they are and how they assisted you.

• References / Bibliography

List any books, magazines, journals, articles, Web sites, scientific databases, and interviews that were important to your research for the experiment.

Science Fairs

Most experiments and projects in this book are followed by Science Project Ideas. This section has great ideas for your science fair project. However, judges at such fairs don't reward projects or experiments that are simply copied from a book. And it doesn't impress judges if your project is too easy: for instance if you examined Isaac Newton's laws of motion by just walking on a plank. But if you put dowels under that plank and learned how Newton's third law of motion really works, then judges would likely give you serious consideration.

Science fair judges tend to reward creative thought and imagination. It is difficult to be creative or imaginative unless you are really interested in your project, so be sure to choose a subject that appeals to you. And before you jump into a project, consider, too, your own talents and the cost of materials you will need.

If you decide to use a project found in this book for a science fair, you should find ways to modify or extend it. This should not be difficult because you'll probably discover that, as you do these projects, new ideas for experiments will come to mind—experiments that could make excellent science fair projects, particularly because the ideas are your own and are interesting to you.

If you decide to enter a science fair and have never done so before, you should read some of the books listed in the Further Reading section. The books with titles that refer to science fairs will provide plenty of helpful hints and information that will enable you to avoid the pitfalls that sometimes plague first-time entrants. You'll learn how to prepare appealing reports that  include charts and graphs, how to set up and display your work, how to present your project, and how to relate to judges and visitors.

Following are some suggestions to consider.

Some Tips for Success at a Science Fair

Science teachers and science fair judges have many different opinions on what makes a good science fair project or experiment. Here are the most important elements:

Originality of Concept is one of the most important things judges consider. Some judges believe that the best science fair projects answer a question that isn't found in a science textbook.

Scientific Content is another main area of evaluation. How was science applied in the procedure? Are there sufficient data? Did you stick to your intended procedure and keep good records?

Thoroughness is next in importance. Was the experiment repeated as often as needed to test your hypothesis? Is your notebook complete, and are the data accurate? Does your research bibliography show you did enough library work?

Clarity in how you present your exhibit shows you had a good understanding of the subject you worked on. It is important that your exhibit clearly presents the results of your work.

Effective Process: Judges recognize that how skillfully you carry out a science fair project is usually more important than its results. A well-done project gives students the best understanding of what scientists actually do day-to-day.

Other points to consider when preparing for your science fair:

The Abstract: Write up a brief explanation of your project and make copies for visitors or judges who want to read it.

Knowledge: Be ready to answer questions from visitors and judges confidently. Know what is in your notebook and make some notes on index cards to remind you of important points.

Practice: Before the science fair begins, prepare a list of several questions you think you might be asked. Think about the answers and about how your display can help to support them. Have a friend or parent ask you questions and answer them out loud. Knowing your work thoroughly helps you feel more confident when you're asked about it.

Appearance: Dress and act in a way that shows you take your project seriously. Visitors and judges should get the impression that you're interested in the project and that you take pride in answering their questions about it.

Remember: Don't block your exhibit. Stand to the side when someone is looking at it.

Safety First

Most of the projects included in this book are perfectly safe. However, the following safety rules are well worth reading before you start any project.

✔ Do any experiments or projects, whether from this book or of your own design, **under the supervision of a science teacher or other knowledgeable adult.**

✔ Read all instructions carefully before proceeding with a project. If you have questions, **check with your supervisor** before going any further. Maintain a serious attitude while conducting experiments. Fooling around can be dangerous to you and to others.

✔ Wear approved goggles (safety glasses) when you are working with a flame or doing anything that might cause injury to your eyes. Goggles can be purchased in hardware or dollar stores.

✔ Do not eat or drink while experimenting.

✔ Have a first-aid kit nearby while you are experimenting.

✔ Do not put your fingers or any object other than properly designed electrical connectors into electrical outlets. Never experiment with household electricity except **under the supervision of a knowledgeable adult.**

✔ Never use a mercury thermometer because exposure to mercury is dangerous; use mercury-free alternatives, such as thermometers containing alcohol.

And now, on to the experiments!

CHAPTER 1

Motion: Measuring Distance and Time

Forces and machines that produce force can put things in motion. Motion is the change in position (location) of a person or thing.

In this chapter you'll learn how scientists study motion. Basically, motion is described by measuring distance and time.

In your work you'll be using metersticks to measure distance, and clocks or stopwatches to measure time. Distances and times can be used to draw graphs that describe motion clearly.

◀ A railway clock in Bern, Switzerland, is positioned above a sign indicating a distance of 100 meters. Swiss measurement of time and distance is famously precise, and trains enter and leave stations on the second.

EXPERIMENT 1.1

Calculating Walking Speed from Distance and Time

Question:

Can you calculate walking speed from distance and time?

Hypothesis:

Walking speed can be estimated by measuring the distance walked and calculating the time it takes to walk that distance.

Materials:

- park, playground, or playing field at least 100 meters (m) long
- group of friends
- metric tape measure or meterstick and string
- markers, such as short stakes
- notebook
- stopwatches or single ordinary watch with a second hand or mode
- graph paper
- pen or pencil
- ruler
- battery-powered toy tractor
- masking tape

Procedure:

1. At a park, playground, or playing field, gather a small group of friends to help mark off a straight line 100 meters (m) long. Divide that line into 10-m segments, as shown in Figure 1.

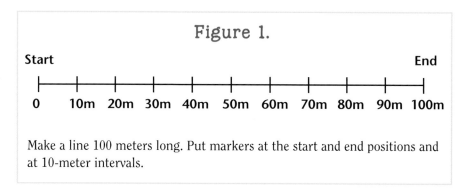

Figure 1.

Start   **End**

0   10m   20m   30m   40m   50m   60m   70m   80m   90m   100m

Make a line 100 meters long. Put markers at the start and end positions and at 10-meter intervals.

This is most easily done using a metric tape measure. Markers, such as short stakes, can be used to indicate the start, end, and 10-m intervals. If you don't have a metric tape, you can use a meterstick and string to make a line 10 m long. If you don't have a meterstick, 10 meters is only about 2 inches short of 11 yards (33 feet).

2. You need to record the times at 10-m intervals as a friend walks along the 100-m-long line. If possible, have people with stopwatches at each 10-m interval.

3. Have the walker stand at the "Start" position. When you shout, "Go," the individual (who could be you) starts walking at an even pace along the line. All ten timers start their watches. As the walker crosses the first 10-m stake, that timer stops his or her watch.

If you can't assemble 10 timers with stopwatches or watches, you can use fewer people and have them move so as to collect data at two or more positions. Or you can collect less accurate data using a single ordinary watch with a second hand or mode.

4. Start the walker at a convenient time. Then move quickly to the 10-m stake. When the walker reaches the 10-m mark, note the time that has elapsed to the nearest second. State that time to a third person, who will record the data. Continue doing this for each 10-m interval until the walker reaches the 100-m stake.

5. When the 100-m walk has been completed, the time for each 10-m interval can be recorded in a data table such as the one shown in Table 1 below.

Results and Conclusions

You can use the data you've collected to make a graph of distance walked versus time. It will resemble the graph shown in Figure 2, which was made using the data in Table 1. As you can see, the recorded times, shown along

Table 1.

Sample Data for a 100-m Walk in Which Times in Seconds (S) are Recorded at 10-m Intervals

Distance walked (m)	Time (s)
0	0.0
10	7.5
20	15.2
30	21.9
40	30.0
50	37.4
60	44.0
70	52.3
80	62.0
90	68.0
100	75.4

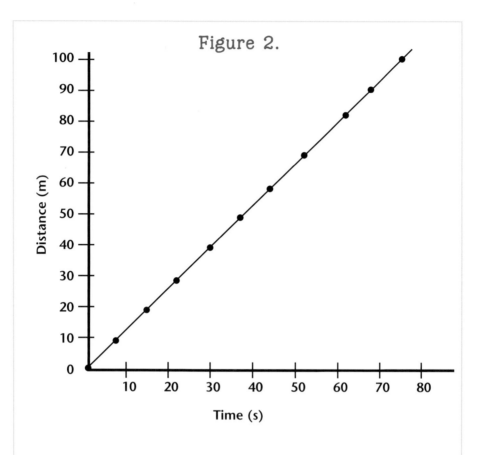

The graph shows distance, in meters (m), versus time, in seconds (s), for a person who walked 100 m.

a horizontal time line or axis, are marked to correspond with each 10-m distance, shown along a vertical axis.

Draw the best straight line you can through the data. Usually, data points don't lie along a perfect straight line because people make errors in recording time, they stop the watch too soon or too late, and, of course, the person may not take exactly the same time to walk each 10-m distance. The best straight line is one that has about as many data points above the line as it has below it.

Figure 3.

The times, taken every 25 cm as a toy vehicle moves along a 2-m-long line, can be recorded and used to make a distance-versus-time graph of the motion.

If you have a battery-powered toy tractor or car like the one shown in Figure 3, you can use it in an experiment. Place strips of masking tape at 25-cm intervals from 0 to 200 centimeters (2 m). Place the toy vehicle on the floor a short distance in front of the start (0) point. Start the toy and record the times the toy passes the 25-cm intervals, starting at 0 and going to 200 cm. Again, use the data to make a distance-versus-time graph for the tractor. How does the tractor graph compare with the walking graph?

 Science Project Ideas

- Repeat the walking experiment using a jogger in place of a walker. How does that change the distance-versus-time graph?

- Using methods similar to those in Experiment 1.1, prepare distance-versus-time graphs of cars moving along a street. Be sure to stand at a safe distance from the street.

EXPERIMENT 1.2

Measuring the Speed of Sound

Question:

What is one way to measure the speed of sound?

Hypothesis:

The speed of sound can be measured by timing the speed of an echo.

Materials:

- building with a large flat wall that will reflect sound
- a long measuring tape
- 2 small boards
- a friend
- stopwatch
- pen or pencil
- paper or notebook

To measure the speed of sound, you can use the echo made by clapping two boards together. An echo is a reflected sound. Find a building with a large flat wall that will reflect sound. You'll also need a partner with a stopwatch.

Procedure:

1. Stand about 50 meters from the building. (Be sure there are no other buildings beside you that will reflect sound.) Clap two small boards together.

   You should hear the echo clearly. The time between clap and echo is too short to measure. However, you can clap the boards together at such a rate that each clap is made at the same time you hear the echo from the previous clap. Then the time between claps will equal the time for the sound to travel *to the building and back to you.*

2. Clap the boards together at this rate. Your partner with a stopwatch should record the time required to make a specific number of claps. After getting your rhythm set, your partner should call zero the clap at which he or she starts timing. Then clap about 40 or more times. Why should the timing start at zero and not at one?

Results and Conclusions

What was the total number of claps the timer counted? How long did it take to make those claps? Use the data you and your partner have collected to find the speed of sound.

Suppose, for example, you were 50 m from the building that reflected the sounds, and you counted 40 claps in 13.2 seconds (s). The time between claps was then

$$\frac{13.2 \text{ s}}{40} = 0.33 \text{ s}$$

The sound must have traveled 100 m (to the building and back) in 0.33 s. According to this data, the speed of sound is

$$\frac{100 \text{ m}}{0.33 \text{ s}} = 303 \text{ m/s}$$

What is the speed of sound according to your data?

 ## Science Project Ideas

- Design and carry out experiments to see if the speed of sound is affected by air temperature.

- Design and carry out experiments to see if sound travels at different speeds in different materials.

- How can you use the speed of sound to determine distance?

- Very careful measurements have determined the speed of light in air to be about 300,000,000 meters (984,000,000 feet) per second. How did scientists measure such a fast speed?

Speed and Slope

The speed at which something moves is the distance it travels divided by the time it takes to go that distance. Using the distance-versus-time graphs you made in Experiment 1.1, it's quite easy to determine the speed at which the walker or toy was moving. The data in Table 1 show that the walker traveled 100 m in 75.4 s. The walker's average speed over that distance was 1.33 meters per second, because

$$\frac{100 \text{ m}}{75.4 \text{ s}} = 1.33 \text{ m/s}$$

The average speed was 1.33 m/s, but if we look at smaller intervals of distance and time, we may find slight differences in speed. For example, the time for the walker to travel from the 30-m marker to the 40-m marker was 30.0 s – 21.9 s, or 8.1 s, which is a speed of

$$\frac{10 \text{ m}}{8.1 \text{ s}} = 1.23 \text{ m/s}$$

On the other hand, the speed while walking from the 80-m to the 90-m marker was

$$\frac{10 \text{ m}}{6.0 \text{ s}} = 1.67 \text{ m/s}$$

Although inaccuracies in measuring times and distances do occur, the data points lie very close to a straight line. Consequently, it's reasonable to say that the walker's speed was very nearly constant (the same) over the 100-m walk.

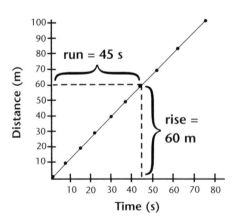

The slope of a graph is the change in the value of the vertical axis (the rise) divided by the corresponding change in the value of the horizontal axis (the run). If you measure the slope of the graph in Figure 2 at any point, you'll find it's 1.33 m/s. For example, according to the slope, after 45 seconds the walker had traveled 60 m. These values for rise and run give a slope of

$$\frac{\text{rise}}{\text{run}} = \frac{60.0 \text{ m}}{45.0 \text{ s}} = 1.33 \text{ m/s}$$

This shows that the walker's average speed during the 100-m walk was 1.33 m/s.

While many times data will yield a graph with a constant slope, such as the one in Figure 2, many other groups of data will not. For each of the distance-versus-time graphs shown in Figure 4, what can you say about the speed during the times shown in the graph?

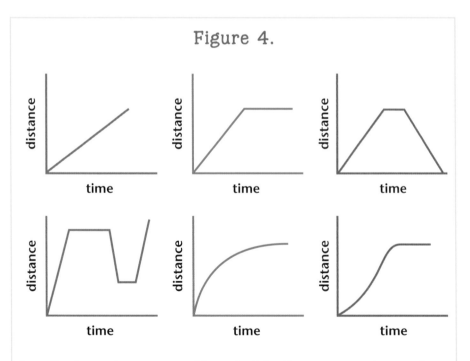

Figure 4.

Describe the motion represented by each of the distance-versus-time graphs. Where on the graphs is speed constant? Where is speed zero? Where is motion reversed? Where is speed decreasing? Increasing?

EXPERIMENT 1.3

Making Velocity-Time Graphs from Distance-Time Graphs

Question:

How can you convert a distance-versus-time graph to a velocity-versus-time graph?

Hypothesis:

If you know the direction of motion in a distance-versus-time graph, the slope of that graph will show the velocity.

Materials:

- distance-versus-time graph (or graphs) from Experiment 1.1
- graph paper
- pen or pencil
- ruler

You may have heard people use the word *velocity* when talking about motion. Velocity is not the same as speed even though both are a measure of distance divided by time. Velocities have a direction as well as a speed. Velocities can be described by arrows (vectors). The length of the arrow is used to indicate the speed; the arrowhead indicates the direction of the motion. What is the velocity indicated by each arrow in Figure 5?

It's easy to convert a distance-versus-time graph to a velocity-versus-time graph. The slope of the distance-versus-time graph gives the speed. If you know the direction of motion, the slope also shows the velocity. Figure 6 shows the velocity-versus-time graph that corresponds to the distance-versus-time graph in Figure 2. The graph shows that the velocity was a constant 1.33 m/s throughout the 75.4-second walk.

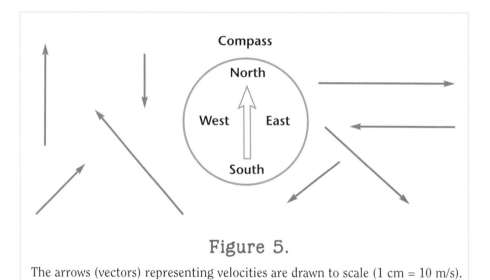

Figure 5.

The arrows (vectors) representing velocities are drawn to scale (1 cm = 10 m/s). Describe the velocity represented by each vector.

Procedure:

1. Use the distance-versus-time graph (or graphs) you drew in Experiment 1.1 to make a velocity-versus-time graph(s). Are your velocity-versus-time graph(s) similar to the one in Figure 6?

If the velocity is constant (doesn't change), the area under the line in a velocity-versus-time graph forms a rectangle, as shown in Figure 6. As you may know, the area of a rectangle is its length times its height. The graph in Figure 6 has a length of 75.4 s and a height of 1.33 m/s.

2. If we multiply its length by its height, we obtain an "area" of very nearly 100 m.

$$1.33 \frac{m}{s} \times 75.4 \ s = 100.3 \ m \ \text{(Notice that} \ \frac{m}{s} \times s = m.)$$

One hundred meters was the distance traveled by the walker whose motion is represented by the graph shown in Figure 2.

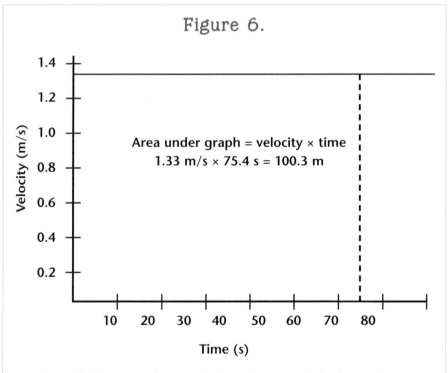

Figure 6.

Area under graph = velocity × time
1.33 m/s × 75.4 s = 100.3 m

The velocity-versus-time graph shown here was obtained from the distance-versus-time graph in Figure 2. Notice that the area of this rectangular graph is equal to the distance traveled in the distance-versus-time graph (Figure 2).

Results and Conclusions

What is the area under the velocity-versus-time graph(s) that you made?
Is it very nearly equal to the distance traveled in the distance-versus-time
graph(s) you made?

 Science Project Idea

- Use the distance-versus-time graphs you made for cars
  along a street to determine the cars' velocities. How
  can you convert these velocities in meters per second
  (m/s) to kilometers per hour (kph)? To miles per hour
  (mph)?

EXPERIMENT 1.4

Accelerated Motion: When Velocity Changes

Question:

Is the velocity of a falling object constant or does it change?

Hypothesis:

The velocity of a falling object will increase as it falls.

Materials:

- metric ruler
- pen or pencil
- graph paper
- calculator

Figure 7 shows on the left a section of tape that was attached to a falling object. The tape fell between the electrodes of a device that produced a spark every 1/60 of a second (every 0.0167 s). Each spark made a hole in the tape. As a result, the distance the object fell during successive 0.0167-second intervals was recorded on the tape. In Figure 7, the holes appear as dots.

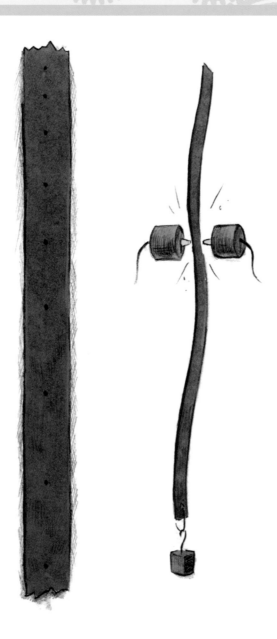

Figure 7.

A falling object pulled a tape through a spark timer. A spark was generated every 1/60 second, leaving a hole in the tape. As a result, the distance the object fell in successive 1/60-s intervals was recorded on the tape. (Tape shown is actual size.)

Procedure:

1. Use Figure 7 to find the velocity of the falling object for each 0.0167-s interval shown. To find the velocity during the first interval, simply divide the distance between the bottom two dots by the time (0.0167 s).

2. Repeat the process to find the velocity for each succeeding interval of 0.0167 s.

3. Plot a graph of the falling object's velocity, in cm/s, versus time. The tape doesn't show the first 3 intervals (3 × 0.0167 s = 0.05 s), during which the object fell 1.23 cm. Consequently, the time axis of your graph should begin at 0.05 s.

   What can you conclude about the velocity of the falling object?

Results and Conclusions

When the velocity of an object changes, we say the object is accelerating. When a car starts from rest, the driver steps on the accelerator and the car's velocity increases, it accelerates. When the driver applies the brakes, the car's velocity decreases. We say it has a negative acceleration, or it decelerates. How do you know that a falling body accelerates?

The acceleration of an object is the rate at which its velocity changes. To find an object's acceleration, you divide its change in velocity by the time it takes for the change to happen.

From the graph you have drawn, you can find the acceleration of a falling object. Previously, you divided the distance traveled by the time it took to travel that distance. That gave you the slope of the distance-versus-time graph, or the object's velocity. In the same way, the slope of a velocity-versus-time graph gives an object's acceleration. Its slope is its change in velocity divided by change in time: its acceleration.

Use the velocity-versus-time graph you have drawn to find the acceleration of a falling object. Since velocity was measured in centimeters per second (cm/s) and time in seconds (s), the acceleration will have the units cm/s ÷ s, which is cm/s/s or cm/s^2. Based on the graph you have drawn, what is the acceleration of a falling body?

How can you use the velocity-versus-time graph you have drawn to find the height through which the body fell during the first 0.15 s of fall?

 Science Project Ideas

- Use the tape from Figure 7 to plot a distance-versus-time graph. What can you say about the slope of the graph you have drawn?

- Design and conduct an experiment of your own to find the acceleration of a falling object.

- Ask an adult to help you find a car's acceleration. Using the speedometer, odometer, and a stopwatch, how can you find the car's acceleration when it starts from rest?

CHAPTER 2

Forces and Motion

In Chapter 1 you experimented with motion and learned how to measure speeds, velocities, and accelerations. But what makes things move? What makes a football fly between the goal posts for an extra point? How can a carpenter drive a nail into a board?

In this chapter you'll investigate forces—pushes and pulls—and see how they are related to motion. You've already seen a force affect movement when you examined the motion of a falling object. As you probably know, objects fall because of gravity—the force that pulls everything, including you, toward Earth.

It was Sir Isaac Newton, an English physicist and mathematician, who developed the laws that explain all the motions we see and experience. Some people believe he saw an apple fall from a tree, and he wondered why it fell. His experiments and observations led him to three basic laws that explain all motion. His first law states that a body at rest will remain at rest unless acted upon by a force. It also states that a body in motion will maintain its velocity unless acted upon by a force. In other words, an object will remain at rest or in motion unless a force acts upon it.

◄ Unless stopped by a goalkeeper, a well-struck soccer ball will remain in motion until it hits the back of the net.

EXPERIMENT 2.1

Testing Newton's First Law

Question:

How can you prove that objects remain at rest if no force acts on them, or will keep moving if no force stops them?

Hypothesis:

Observing your own use of everyday toys and tools reveals the principles of Newton's first law of motion.

Materials:

- **an adult**
- bottle with a small mouth
- smooth table
- index card about 4 cm x 6 cm (1.5 in x 2.5 in)
- marble
- small plastic sheet
- plastic cup
- water
- Superball toy ball
- doll
- toy truck
- board
- brick
- rubber bands
- air-hockey table and puck
- piece of cardboard
- spool
- round balloon
- sharp knife
- finishing nail
- glue
- sharp pencil
- twist-tie
- smooth, level, Formica counter

Most people have no difficulty accepting Newton's statement that bodies at rest remain at rest. You can easily prove to yourself that in the absence of a force, objects remain at rest.

Procedure:

1. Put a bottle with a small mouth on a smooth table.

2. Place a small piece of an index card, about 4 cm x 6 cm (1.5 in x 2.5 in), on the mouth of the bottle.

3. Put a marble on the card so that it's centered over the mouth of the bottle (Figure 8a).

4. Snap your finger against one edge of the card. The card will sail away, leaving the marble on the bottle's mouth.

Results and Conclusions

The force of your finger struck the card, not the marble. Because the card and the marble weren't connected, the marble remained at rest.

Here are other ways to prove Newton's first law of motion.

Procedure:

1. Place a plastic sheet on a smooth table.

2. Put a plastic cup half filled with water on the sheet.

3. Holding one side of the plastic sheet in both hands, quickly jerk it downward and outward (Figure 8b). The cup of water will be left on the table.

4. Walk along an uncarpeted hallway or some other long, hard-surfaced floor carrying a Superball. As you walk, drop the ball (Figure 8c).

Figure 8.

Ways of testing Newton's first law of motion.

It will, of course, bounce off the floor. Do you have to stop to catch it, or can you keep walking and catch it? What happens if you stop walking at the moment you drop the ball? How does this experiment illustrate Newton's first law?

5. Place a doll on a toy truck at the top of a board set at an incline.

6. Let the truck roll down the incline and crash into a heavy object such as a brick (Figure 8d). What happens to the toy truck? What happens to the doll? How does this experiment illustrate Newton's first law?

7. Repeat the experiment, but this time fasten the doll to the truck with rubber bands. What happens this time? Why do you think cars and trucks have seat belts?

8. You can come even closer to observing the kind of ongoing motion Newton imagined by watching a puck slide across the surface of a level air-hockey table. Give the puck a slight push and watch it continue to move.

Results and Conclusions

What do you notice about the puck's speed? Its direction of motion? Does it seem to demonstrate the first law of motion? When does it change direction? How can you explain its change in direction?

Here is an experiment you can do to study velocity. You can build an air car, which behaves like an air-hockey puck. You'll need a piece of cardboard, a spool, and a balloon as shown in Figure 9.

Procedure:

1. **Ask an adult** to use a sharp knife to cut out a square piece of cardboard about 4 to 5 inches on a side.

Figure 9.

You can make an air car from very simple materials.

Materials

2. Push a finishing nail through the center of the smooth bottom of the square and remove the nail. Then glue an empty spool (one on which thread was wound) on the top side of the square. The hole in the spool should be aligned with the hole in the cardboard square. If the hole through the spool is covered with paper, push a sharp pencil through the paper. You should be able to see through the spool.

3. After the glue has dried, blow up a round balloon. Tie the neck of the balloon with a twist-tie and attach it to the spool by stretching the end of the balloon neck over the top of the spool.

4. Place the air car on a smooth, level, Formica counter and remove the twist-tie.

5. Give the air car a gentle push, and it should slide along the counter at nearly constant speed. If it does not slide smoothly, use a sharp pencil to widen the hole through the bottom of the cardboard, or remove any roughness along the edges of the cardboard. Then try it again.

6. Once you're able to make the air car move at a steady speed along the surface, give it a second push in the direction it's moving.

7. Repeat the experiment, but this time have the second push oppose the car's motion.

Results and Conclusions

What happens to the car's velocity when a force pushes it in the direction it's moving? When the force opposes the motion?

 Science Project Idea

- Design other ways to demonstrate Newton's first law of motion.

EXPERIMENT 2.2

Friction and Newton's First Law

Question:

What is the main force acting to slow something down or change its direction?

Hypothesis:

Friction is the most common force that affects motion.

Materials:

- 4 or more smooth, wood blocks of the same size (You may wish to **ask an adult** to cut them from a length of 2-inch x 4-inch lumber, and then you can smooth them with sandpaper.)
- large board
- table or counter
- sensitive spring scale or small weights, such as identical washers, string, and pulley or
- paper clip
- wide rubber bands
- felt pads
- thumbtacks
- aluminum foil, wax paper, and plastic wrap (optional)
- Masonite board, chipboard, a kitchen counter, linoleum, other surfaces
- small wooden dowels or round pencils
- toy truck

As you saw in the different parts of Experiment 2.1, when a force is applied to an object at rest or in motion, its velocity changes. The object accelerates because its velocity increases, decreases, or changes direction.

You may be less willing to accept the second part of Newton's first law about a moving body maintaining its velocity unless acted upon by a force. For example, if you place a book on the floor and give it a push, it doesn't maintain its motion. It comes to rest; it stops! However, the book is actually obeying Newton's law.

Newton would have told you why a book sliding across a floor doesn't continue to move as the first law predicts it should. Remember, bodies continue to move unless acted upon by a force. The force that brings a sliding book to rest is a force known as friction. You can measure the force of friction.

Procedure:

1. Place a smooth wooden block on a smooth, level surface such as a large board on a table or counter.

2. Pull the block with a sensitive spring scale, as shown in Figure 10a, so that it moves at a slow, steady velocity. Since its velocity is not changing, the force you're applying to pull the block just equals the force of friction. The reading on the spring scale is the force of friction.

3. If you don't have a sensitive spring scale, you can use small weights, such as identical washers, to pull on the block (see Figure 10b).

4. A small pulley will allow you to pass a string attached to the block over the table. You can then tie an opened paper clip to the string and add weights. If you don't have a pulley, you can use a bent paper clip to support the string as shown.

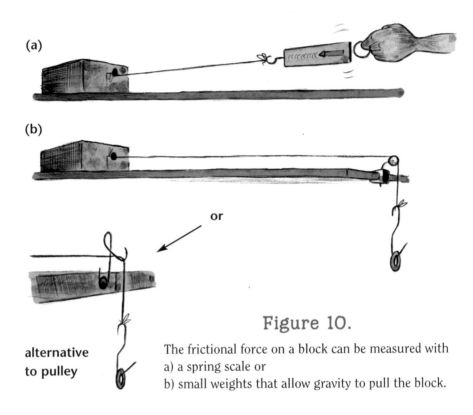

(a)

(b)

or

alternative to pulley

Figure 10.

The frictional force on a block can be measured with
a) a spring scale or
b) small weights that allow gravity to pull the block.

Should you want to know the actual force, you can weigh the washers on a balance. Because it takes a little more force to make the block start to slide than to keep it sliding once in motion, you should tap the board with your finger after adding a weight.

To make the block accelerate, you need to pull with more force. The total force applied minus the force of friction is the "net force." Scientists use a unit called a newton to measure force. The abbreviation for a newton is N. A newton is the force needed to make one kilogram accelerate at a rate of one meter per second per second.

Procedure:

1. To see how the kind of surface affects friction, you can prepare blocks with different surfaces, as shown in Figure 11. Leave one block unchanged.

2. Put wide rubber bands on a second block, felt pads on a third, and push thumbtacks into another. The thumbtacks will go in easier if you use a second block to press them in, as shown in the drawing.

3. You might also prepare surfaces using aluminum foil, wax paper, or plastic wrap.

4. Compare the frictional force on these different surfaces as they move at constant speed. On which surface is the friction greatest? On which is friction the least? List the surfaces in order of decreasing friction.

5. Try pulling the same blocks over a surface other than the wood board you have been using. You might use both sides of a Masonite board, a piece of chipboard, a kitchen counter, linoleum, and other surfaces.

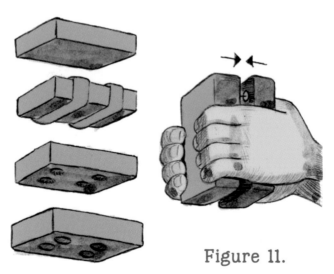

Figure 11.

Does the kind of surface affect the amount of friction?

Results and Conclusions

Does the surface on which the blocks slide affect the force of friction? Does it affect the order of the blocks on the list you made?

Does weight affect friction? Let's find out.

Procedure:

1. Double the weight of a block by placing a second block on the first.

2. Again, measure the force needed to make the two blocks move at a steady speed. How does the force required to move a stack of two blocks compare with the force needed for a single block?

3. Predict the force needed to pull a stack of three blocks along the same surface. Try it! Was your prediction correct?

4. To test the effect of surface area on friction, hook two blocks together like a train. You already know the force needed to move the two blocks when they are stacked. Now you can keep the weight the same but change the area over which the friction acts.

Results and Conclusions

What have you done to the total surface area in contact with the board or table by making the two blocks into a train?

Measure the force needed to move the two-block train at a steady speed. How does the force compare with the force needed to move a stack of two blocks with half as much surface area? Repeat the experiment using three blocks. How does the force needed to move a three-block train compare with the force needed to move a stack of three blocks?

What can you conclude about the effect of weight on friction? About the effect of surface area on friction?

Procedure:

1. Measure the force needed to pull a stack of three or four blocks along a smooth, level surface.

2. Then place the blocks on a series of small wooden dowels or round pencils, as shown in Figure 12. Measure the force needed to make the blocks move along the rollers. How does "rolling friction" compare with "sliding friction"?

3. Place a toy truck upside down on the stack of blocks you just used. Measure the force needed to pull the blocks and truck along a board.

4. Next, turn the truck right-side up so that its wheels are on the board. Put the blocks on the toy truck and measure the force needed to make the truck move. Notice that the total weight is the same in both cases.

Figure 12.

Do rollers reduce friction?

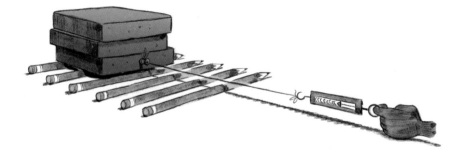

Results and Conclusions

What effect do wheels have on friction?

 Science Project Ideas

- If you use thumbtacks for the block's surface, what can you do to change the surface area in contact with the material over which it slides? Does doubling the thumbtack surface area affect the force needed to overcome friction?

- How can you change the surface area of contact for a rubber-band surface on a block? Does the amount of rubber surface affect the force needed to overcome friction?

- Treat two large paperback books as two decks of cards and shuffle their pages together. After shuffling the pages, push the books as closely together as possible. Now try to pull the books apart. How can you explain your inability to do so?

Newton's Second Law of Motion

Newton's second law states that when a force is applied to an object, the object will accelerate in the direction of the force. When you push on a door, it opens in front of you. Newton added to the second law a rule about how the size of the force and the heaviness of the object affects acceleration. He said that the bigger the force, the bigger will be the object's acceleration. The heavier the object, the smaller will be its acceleration. To make a heavy object and a light object move side by side, you have to pull harder on the heavier object.

Newton's second law applies only to the net force, the amount of the force that is greater than the force of friction. The rule that acceleration is related to force means that doubling the net force will double the acceleration, tripling the net force will triple the acceleration, and so on. That acceleration and mass are related means that doubling the mass will halve the acceleration, tripling the mass will reduce the acceleration to one-third, and so on.

The mass of an object can be determined on an equal-arm balance. Mass is usually measured in grams (g) or kilograms (kg). A kilogram of sand has the same mass as a kilogram of water, even though the sand takes up less space. If you place a kilogram of sand and a kilogram of water on opposite balance pans, the balance beam will be level.

EXPERIMENT 2.3

Detecting Acceleration

Question:

How can you tell if a moving object is accelerating?

Hypothesis:

You can build a simple instrument that will respond to accelerated motion.

Materials:

- jar (about a pint or half pint) with screw-on cap
- thread
- T-pin
- tape
- water

- cork or another light material
- clear vial or test tube and cap or cork
- soap
- level table or counter

In Chapter 1 you found that to calculate an object's acceleration you need to know its change in velocity over a certain length of time. It's easy to tell whether or not some objects are accelerating. All you need is a very simple instrument that you can build. It's called an accelerometer (ak sell eh ROM eh ter). Figure 13 shows two types of accelerometers that you can build with materials that are readily available. Use simple observation to determine the direction of the acceleration.

Figure 13.

(a)

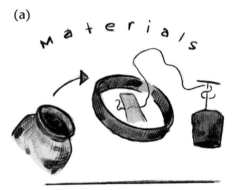

(b)

air
bubble

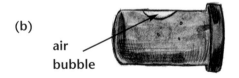

You can make accelerometers
from simple materials.

Procedure:

1. To build the jar accelerometer, attach one end of a length of thread to a T-pin.

2. Securely tape the other end of the thread to the jar's screw-on cap.

3. Push the T-pin into a cork or another light material such as a piece of Styrofoam. Make sure the thread is not so long that the cork will rub against the bottom of the jar.

4. Fill the jar with water, screw on the cap assembly, and invert the jar (see Figure 13a).

5. To make the vial or test-tube accelerometer, fill the tube with water, leaving just enough space for a small bubble of air. Add a tiny piece of soap. The soap will prevent the bubble from sticking to the vial's surface.

6. Cap the vial, or cork the test tube, and lay it on its side (see Figure 13b).

7. To see how these instruments respond to accelerated motion, place them on a level table or counter. Pull each one so that it accelerates.

Results and Conclusions

Notice that the cork or bubble always moves in the direction of the acceleration, which is also the direction of the force. When you start from rest and pull the accelerometer forward, the cork or bubble moves forward. How can you make the bubble or cork move just a little bit? How can you make it move a lot?

When the accelerometer slows and finally stops, the force (usually friction) opposes the motion. The acceleration is negative (deceleration) because the velocity gets smaller. The cork or bubble moves the other way, opposite the motion, but, as always, in the direction of the force.

Carry an accelerometer with you as you walk. Do you accelerate and decelerate while walking?

Save the accelerometers you have built. You'll use them in some later experiments in this book.

EXPERIMENT 2.4

Testing Newton's Second Law of Motion

Question:
Can you observe the effects of forces that oppose motion?

Hypothesis:
The simple accelerometer and a spring scale can be used to measure the effects of force (including friction) on moving objects.

Materials:

- child's wagon
- accelerometer from Experiment 2.3
- smooth, level surface
- 0-2,000-gram (0-20-newton) spring scale
- heavy weights, such as concrete blocks, pails of sand, or some other heavy objects that can be easily duplicated

Procedure:

1. Place a weight in a child's wagon. You might use a concrete block, a pail of sand, or some other heavy object that you can find more than one of. Attach to the wagon one of the accelerometers you built in Experiment 2.3.

2. Use a spring scale to pull the wagon along a smooth, level surface at a slow, constant (unchanging) speed. The spring scale allows you to measure the force on the wagon.

Results and Conclusions

What is the reading on the spring scale when the wagon moves at a steady speed? What does the accelerometer indicate? What is the frictional force between the wagon's wheels and the floor? (See Experiment 2.2.) What happens if the force you apply to the wagon is less than the frictional force?

What happens when the force you use to pull the wagon is greater than the frictional force? Let's find out.

Procedure:

1. Use the spring scale to pull the wagon with a force twice as large as the frictional force.

2. Keep the spring stretched to that force as you pull the wagon along the smooth, level surface. What happens to the wagon's velocity as you continue to pull it with this constant force? What does the accelerometer indicate?

   What do you think will happen if you use the spring scale to apply a force three or four times as big as the frictional force? Try it! What does the accelerometer indicate? Were you right?

3. Next, increase the weight in the wagon by adding a second concrete block, pail of sand, or whatever you're using as a weight.

4. Measure the force needed to move the wagon along at a steady speed. Does weight affect the friction between the wagon's wheels and the surface?

5. Now pull on this heavier wagon with the same *net force* you applied to the lighter wagon. Remember, the net force is the total force minus the force of friction. For example, if you pulled on the wagon with a force 200 g (2.0 newtons) greater than the force of friction when you had one unit of weight in the wagon, do the same now that there are two units of weight in the wagon. That is, pull with a force 2.0 newtons greater than the frictional force on the wagon. You want the net force—the total force applied minus the frictional force—to be the same as it was with one unit of weight in the wagon.

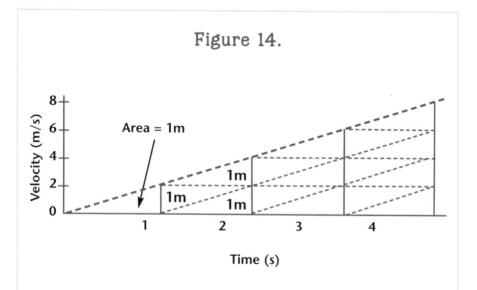

Figure 14.

This velocity-versus-time graph shows a constant acceleration. The velocity increases by the same amount (2 m/s) every second. As you learned in Chapter 1, the area under a velocity-versus-time graph gives the distance traveled. In the graph, each little triangle is equal to one meter. (Remember, the area of a triangle is one-half the base times the altitude.) After one second, the object had gone 1 m; after two seconds, it had gone 4 m. How far had it gone after three seconds? After four seconds?

Results and Conclusions

Does the added weight in the wagon affect the rate at which the wagon's speed increases under the same force? If it does, how does it affect it?

You have seen that the wagon accelerates (increases its speed) when you apply a force greater than the force of friction, which opposes its motion. You have seen, too, that the acceleration is greater when the force is greater and smaller when the mass is increased.

 Science Project Ideas

- It's difficult, even with the accelerometer, to tell by simply observing whether or not an acceleration is constant—that is, whether or not the speed increases by the same amount during each succeeding second. However, as you can see from Figure 14, if acceleration is constant, the distance traveled will be proportional to the square of the time traveled. A wagon moving with constant acceleration will move four times as far in two units of time as it does in one unit of time. If it goes 1 meter in 1 second, it will go 4 meters in 2 seconds, 9 meters in 3 seconds, and so on.

- Design an experiment to find out if the wagon moves at constant acceleration when you apply a constant force. You'll probably want someone to help you with the experiment. You'll also find it helpful to choose a force that exceeds friction by a small rather than a large amount.

EXPERIMENT 2.5

Galileo's Investigation of Acceleration Due to Gravity

Question:

Could scientists of long ago study acceleration even though they had no technical instruments to help them?

Hypothesis:

Yes. Their observations and practical experiments with the force of gravity helped them understand forces and motion.

Materials:

- 2 balls that have different weights, such as a baseball and a tennis ball
- straight, rigid, 3-m section of aluminum or steel angle (V-shaped length of metal that can be obtained from a hardware store)
- wood blocks or books
- meterstick
- marker
- hard rubber or large steel ball
- stopwatch
- pencil
- paper or notebook
- calculator
- graph paper
- string
- tape
- 5 large marbles
- metal tray (optional)

Using Figure 7, you found the acceleration of a falling object. Galileo, an Italian scientist born in 1564, lived long before spark timers were invented. Yet he did a number of experiments to measure the acceleration caused by gravity and to show that the acceleration was the same for all masses. You can do experiments similar to his.

Procedure:

1. Take two balls that have different masses, such as a baseball and a tennis ball. Hold them the same height above the floor and release them at the same time. Do they fall together and strike the floor at the same time? Or does the heavier ball fall faster?

   Galileo performed a similar experiment to disprove an ancient theory that claimed an object twice as heavy would fall twice as fast. According to legend, Galileo dropped two cannonballs, one ten times heavier than the other, from the Leaning Tower of Pisa. They both struck the ground at very nearly the same time.

   Galileo believed objects accelerate as they fall. However, he had no way to measure the short time intervals needed to find the change in speed of falling objects. Therefore, he diluted gravity by letting a ball roll down an inclined plane. It was still gravity that pulled the ball down the incline, but the ball rolled so slowly that he could measure its acceleration. You can build a version of Galileo's inclined plane.

2. Find a straight, rigid, 3-m section of aluminum or steel angle. Lay it on a floor with the V facing upward.

3. Elevate one end about 15 cm with pieces of wood or books. This produces an angle of incline of about 3 degrees.

4. Mark off 20-cm intervals starting from the elevated end. A hard rubber or steel ball can serve as the "falling body."

5. With a stopwatch, measure the times it takes for the ball to roll from rest at the starting point (0 distance) to each marked distance along the incline. When you release the ball, be careful not to give it any backspin. This is best done by putting a pencil across the front of the ball. To release the ball, simply pull the pencil forward quickly.

6. Make several runs for each distance. Record your results and find the average time for each distance.

Results and Conclusions

According to Galileo, the distance the ball "fell" should be proportional to the square of the time it fell. You can check to see if this is true. For each set of distance-time data you recorded, divide the distance by the time squared. If they are proportional, all the quotients should be about the same. For example, suppose the ball rolled 10 cm in 2 seconds and 40 cm in 4 seconds, then

$$\frac{10 \text{ cm}}{2s \times 2s} = 2.5 \text{ cm/s}^2, \text{ and } \frac{40 \text{ cm}}{4s \times 4s} = 2.5 \text{ cm/s}^2$$

Since the quotients are the same (or nearly so), we can conclude that the distances are proportional to the times squared.

Plot a graph of distance traveled versus the square of the time to travel that distance. If distance is proportional to time squared, the points you graph should lie close to a straight line. What happens to the acceleration if you make the incline steeper?

Of course, Galileo did not have a stopwatch. He measured time by letting water fall from a vessel with a very narrow opening. The volume of water collected during the time the ball rolled was his measurement of time.

Modern timing devices can measure very small time intervals. Experiments using these devices show that over a few meters objects do fall with constant acceleration. Because Earth's gravity varies slightly from place to place, the actual value of the acceleration depends slightly on location. At the equator, the acceleration is about 9.8 m/s/s. When falling objects reach high speeds, friction with the air can be as great as the force of gravity. When this occurs, the body no longer accelerates downward but reaches a *terminal velocity*, that is, a speed that doesn't get any bigger. This is what happens to skydivers who jump out of airplanes. They spread their bodies out to increase contact with the air and reach a terminal velocity of about 190 kph (120 mph).

Following is another way to check for constant acceleration.

Procedure:

1. Cut a piece of string 1.7 m (170 cm) long.

2. Tape five large marbles along its length. The first marble is to be taped to the lower end and will rest on the floor. Tape the second marble 10 cm from the first. Tape the third 40 cm from the first, the fourth 90 cm from the first, and the fifth 160 cm from the first.

Results and Conclusions

Notice that the distances from the bottom marble to the others increases by 1:4:9:16, which is the same as 12: 22: 32: 42. When you hold the string vertically and then release it, what should be true about the times between the sounds you hear when the marbles strike the floor? If you have difficulty hearing the sounds, let the marbles fall on a metal tray.

 ## Science Project Ideas

- Do some research to find Galileo's description of his experiment using the inclined plane. Then see if you can, as closely as possible, duplicate his equipment and his results.

- Tape a metal washer to the exact center of an index card. Tape an identical washer to one end of another index card. Hold both cards facedown at the same height above the floor. Release them at the same time. Which card reaches the floor first? Why does one card fall faster than the other?

ⓥ EXPERIMENT 2.6

Testing Newton's Third Law of Motion

Question:

Can you actually experience the law that for every action there is an equal and opposite reaction?

Hypothesis:

You can use a skateboard to see how Newton's third law works.

Materials:

- **2 adults**
- 2 skateboards
- large, smooth, level floor
- a friend about your size
- thin rope
- a heavy person and a light person
- oblong balloon
- twist-tie
- long string
- soda straw
- clear tape
- glass of water
- a balance
- clay
- weights or another glass of water if a balance other than an electronic one is used
- spring balance
- sharp pencil
- Styrofoam cup
- scissors
- 2 flexible drinking straws
- thread
- water
- long plank
- wooden dowels

Newton's Laws of Motion

According to Newton's third law, for every action there is always an equal and opposite reaction. This law might be called the "push, push-back law." What it means is that if you push something or someone in one direction, that person or thing will push back on you with an equal force in the opposite direction.

Procedure:

1. Find two skateboards and a large, smooth, level floor, such as a long hallway.

2. Ask a friend who is about your size to sit on one skateboard. Seat yourself on a second skateboard behind your friend.

3. Reach out and push on your friend's back. What happens?

4. Place the two skateboards several meters apart. Have a friend sit on one skateboard holding one end of a thin rope. Seat yourself on the other skateboard and hold the other end of the rope.

5. Pull on the rope and see what happens.

6. Try again, but this time have your friend pull on the rope.

What happens to your friend? What happens to you? Did you accelerate? Did your friend accelerate? How is this experiment a test of Newton's third law of motion? What happened when you pulled on the rope? Was your prediction correct? What happened when your friend pulled on the rope?

Next we'll combine Newton's second and third laws and test the third law in other ways.

Procedure:

1. Suppose a heavy person sits on one skateboard and a light person sits on the second. Remembering Newton's second law of motion, what do you predict will happen when one of the two pushes on the other? Try it! Was your prediction correct? Will the result be similar if one person pulls on the other?

2. Blow up an oblong balloon and seal the neck with a twist-tie. Tie one end of a long string to a point high in a room. Run the other end of the string through a soda straw.

3. Tape the balloon to the straw, as shown in Figure 15a. Hold the free end of the string taut as you remove the twist-tie and release the balloon. What happens? How does this experiment illustrate Newton's third law?

4. Place a glass of water on a balance pan. Depending on the type of balance, balance the glass of water with weights, another glass of water, or, if it's an electronic balance, simply note the weight.

5. Attach a large ball of clay to one end of a string. Then attach the other end to a spring balance. Predict what will happen to the weight of the clay and to the weight of the glass of water when you lower the clay into the water as shown in Figure 15b. Try it! Were you right? Did the clay push on the water? Did the water push on the clay? How is this experiment a test of Newton's third law?

6. Using a sharp pencil, make two small holes near the bottom on opposite sides of a Styrofoam cup.

7. With scissors, cut the ends from two flexible drinking straws. Push the ends through the holes in the cup and flex the straws as shown in Figure 15c. Next, make two small holes on opposite sides near the top of the cup. Run a piece of thread through both holes. Tie the ends to make a loop. Support the cup with a second piece of thread tied to the loop.

8. Fill the cup with water and watch the water "jet" out from the straws.

What happens to the cup? How does this experiment illustrate Newton's third law?

9. After the cup has emptied, turn one of the straw jets around so that it points in the opposite direction.

Results and Conclusions

Predict what will happen when you repeat the experiment. Were you right?

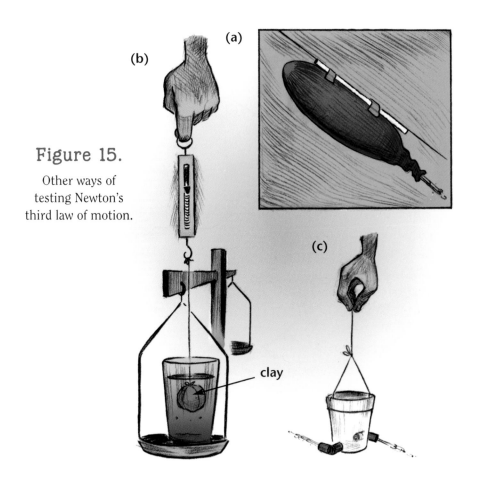

Figure 15.

Other ways of testing Newton's third law of motion.

(a)

(b)

(c)

clay

Walking and Newton's Third Law

Think about what happens when you walk. As your foot bends, it pushes back against the ground (Earth). The ground provides an equal but opposite force that pushes you forward. Of course, friction is an essential force in walking. Have you ever tried to walk on an icy surface? If you have, you found that your foot could no longer exert a large force on the ground.

You can do an experiment to see what happens when you walk and why friction is an essential part of walking.

Figure 16.

How does "walking the plank" illustrate Newton's third law of motion?

Procedure:

1. Place a long plank on a smooth, level floor. Consider the forces you exert on the plank as you walk.

2. Now put the plank on some wooden dowels as shown in Figure 16.

3. **Ask two adults**, one on either side of you, to support you as you start to walk along the plank.

Results and Conclusions

Explain what happens to the plank as you walk. Remember, the plank is on rollers. You can no longer push against the ground. How does this experiment demonstrate Newton's third law of motion?

 Science Project Ideas

- Devise other experiments to test Newton's third law of motion.

- If Earth and the sun attract each other with equal and opposite gravitational forces, what keeps Earth and the sun from coming together?

CHAPTER 3

Pendulums and Springs: Oscillating Motion

The types of motion you examined in Chapters 1 and 2 were along straight lines on flat surfaces. Of course, not all motion is along straight lines or on flat surfaces. Regardless of direction or location, however, Newton's laws hold true.

In this chapter, you'll investigate objects that move back and forth and up and down. Pendulums, springs, and projectiles move in these ways.

◄ A bungee jumper free falls from the Gouritz River Bridge in South Africa. The elastic bungee cord, which works like a spring, must be stretched an exact distance before springing back to its original length.

EXPERIMENT 3.1

Pendulums Move Back and Forth

Question:

Does a pendulum bob's mass or the distance it swings affect the pendulum's period?

Hypothesis:

No, a bob's mass and amplitude do not affect a pendulum's period.

Materials:

- **an adult**
- sharp knife or razor blade
- tongue depressor or coffee stirrer
- thread
- heavy metal washers
- tape
- meterstick
- drawing compass
- high surface such as the top of a refrigerator, shelf, or door frame
- stopwatch or a watch that can measure seconds
- pen or pencil
- paper
- metric ruler

While seated in church one day, Galileo fixed his eye on a chandelier. The chandelier, set into motion by the force of air currents, was swinging slowly back and forth. Using his pulse as a timer, Galileo found that the time for the chandelier to make one full swing seemed to be constant regardless of how far it swung. After reaching his home, he carried out an experiment to see if the swing time really was constant. You can do a similar experiment.

To carry out Galileo's experiment, you can build a simple pendulum. A pendulum (from the Latin word *pendere*, "to hang") is made up of a weight suspended from a fixed point so that it can swing freely. The weight is called a bob. You have probably seen one type of pendulum in a grandfather clock.

Procedure:

1. **Ask an adult** to use a sharp knife or razor blade to make a slit about 2 cm long at one end of a tongue depressor or coffee stirrer, as shown in Figure 17.

2. Slide one end of a long piece of thread into the slit. Then tape the tongue depressor to a high surface such as the top of a refrigerator, a shelf, or a door frame.

3. Tie the other end of the string to a heavy metal washer. The washer will serve as the pendulum bob. Move the thread up or down until the distance between the bottom of the tongue depressor and the *center* of the washer is exactly 1.0 m (39⅜ in).

4. Tape the upper end of the string to the tongue depressor so that the length will not change when the bob swings.

5. Pull the washer several centimeters to one side and release it.

6. Use a stopwatch or a watch that can measure seconds to find the time for the bob to make 10 complete swings.

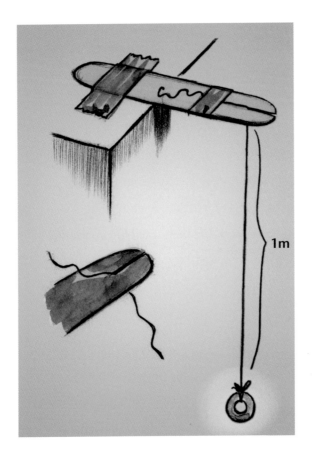

Figure 17.

You can build a simple pendulum to duplicate one of Galileo's experiments.

Results and Conclusions

The period of a pendulum is the time to make one complete swing, from one side to the other and back. What is the period of the pendulum you have made? Why do you think it's more accurate to find the period by measuring 10 swings and dividing by 10 rather than timing just one swing?

What do you calculate the period to be if you measure the time for the pendulum to make 20 swings? Does the period of a pendulum seem to be constant, as Galileo saw it was?

When you pull a pendulum bob to one side, you also raise it by a small amount. When you release it, the force of gravity causes it to accelerate as it returns to its original lower position. (In the same way, a toy truck will roll down an incline.) Since the bob is moving when it reaches its original position, it continues to move beyond its rest position. As it rises on the other side of its swing, gravity again pulls on it, causing it to decelerate, come to a stop, and swing back.

How high do you think it rises on the other side of its swing compared to the height of the release point? The swing certainly looks symmetrical, so you might think it rises to the same height on both sides of its swing. One way to check is to put your nose against the bob before you release it. Don't move. Does the bob return to very nearly the point from which you released it?

Now test the effect of mass on a pendulum. Will the mass of the bob affect the period of a pendulum?

Procedure:

1. Tape a second washer to the first one so that they are side by side. Does doubling the mass change the period? What do you think the period will be if you triple the mass by taping a third washer to the bob? Try it! Did you predict correctly?

   Now test the effect of amplitude on a pendulum. The amplitude of a pendulum is the distance it swings from its rest position.

2. Pull the pendulum bob 1.0 cm from its rest position. Release it and measure the period by timing 10 or more swings.

5. Measure the period when the pendulum bob is displaced 2, 4, and then 8 cm from its rest position. What is the effect of amplitude on the period of a pendulum?

The half-life of a pendulum can be defined as the time required for its amplitude to decrease by half. You can determine a pendulum's half-life.

Procedure:

1. Build a pendulum so that the bob is very close to the floor.

2. Make a dot at the center of a sheet of paper. Then use a drawing compass to make circles with radii of 10 cm, 5 cm, and 2.5 cm.

3. With your pendulum at rest, tape the paper to the floor so that the bob's center is directly over the center of the circles.

4. Pull the bob to the side until it's at the edge of the largest circle, 10 cm from the circle's center. Release the bob and count the number of swings required for the bob to lose half its amplitude.

5. Stop counting when the bob swings out only to the 5-cm circle. Record the number of swings, which you can define as the pendulum's half-life.

6. Repeat the experiment to see how many swings are required for the pendulum's amplitude to decrease from 5 cm to 2.5 cm.

Results and Conclusions

How does this half-life compare with the first one you measured? Design an experiment of your own to see how the mass of the bob affects the half-life of a pendulum.

Save your pendulum for the next experiment.

 Science Project Ideas

- Investigate further the effect of amplitude on the period of a pendulum by continuing to increase the amplitude to its maximum value. What do you find?

- When did clock makers recognize that pendulums could be used as clocks? What modifications did they have to make for such clocks to be practical?

- What is a Foucault pendulum? What is its significance? Perhaps you would like to build one.

EXPERIMENT 3.2

Pendulums of Different Lengths

Question:

Can you change a pendulum's period?

Hypothesis:

By changing the length of a pendulum, you can change its period.

Materials:

- **an adult**
- pendulum from previous experiment
- meterstick
- graph paper
- drinking straw
- pencil
- drill
- stopwatch or a watch that can measure seconds
- second pendulum like one from previous experiment
- nail or hook

Use the simple pendulum you built in the previous experiment to investigate the effect of length on the period of a pendulum.

Procedure:

1. Use a stopwatch or a watch that can measure seconds to accurately measure the period.

2. You can change the pendulum's length by pulling the thread through the slit in the tongue depressor. What is the period for the following lengths: 1.00 m, 0.75 m, 0.50 m, 0.25 m, 1.50 m, and, if possible, 2.00 m?

3. Record the data you collect for each length.

Results and Conclusions

Does the period change when the length changes? Does halving the length of a pendulum halve its period? Does doubling the length double the period? What happens to the period when the length is one-quarter as large? What happens to the period when the length is four times as great?

Plot a graph of the pendulum's period versus its length. Does the graph appear to be a straight line?

Next, plot a graph of the period squared versus the length. Do the points of this graph lie reasonably close to a straight line?

What do the graphs tell you about the relationship between a pendulum's period and its length?

Next, we'll study "coupled pendulums."

Procedure:

1. Build another simple pendulum like the one made in Experiment 3.1 and mount the two side by side, as shown in Figure 18a. Use a drinking straw to connect the two pendulums.

2. Pull one of the bobs to one side in a direction parallel to the straw. Release the bob and watch. What happens over time? What force causes the motion to be transferred from one bob to the other? Repeat the experiment with the straw closer to the bobs, as shown in Figure 18bi.

(a)

Figure 18.

a) Couple two pendulums with a drinking straw. Pull one bob to the side and release it. Watch and wait. What happens to the motion?

b) What happens if you i) lower the straw? ii) tilt the straw? iii) shorten one pendulum? iv) start the bob with back-and-forth rather than side-to-side motion?

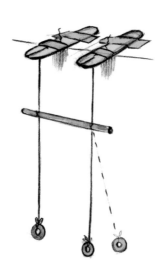

(i)   (ii)   (iii)   (iv)

(b)

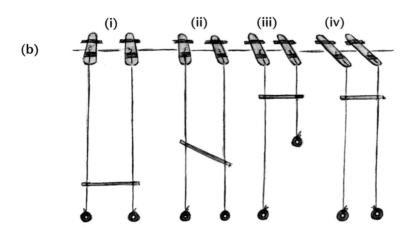

Results and Conclusions

How does moving the straw affect the motion? What happens to the motions of the bobs if the straw is tilted (Figure 18bii)? What happens to the motions if one pendulum is longer than the other (Figure 18biii)? What happens if the bob is released so that it swings in a direction perpendicular to the straw (Figure 18biv)?

A physical pendulum is one made from a single piece of rigid material, such as the pendulum in a grandfather clock. You can make a physical pendulum from a meterstick.

Procedure:

1. Find a meterstick with a hole close to one end or **ask an adult** to drill a hole very close to the end of one.

2. Hang the pendulum from a nail or hook. Pull it to one side and release it.

Results and Conclusions

What is the period of this pendulum? What would be the length of a simple pendulum with the same period as the physical pendulum you just built?

 Science Project Ideas

- From what you know about gravity and falling objects, why would you expect the period of a pendulum not to be affected by the weight of the bob?

- As you know, falling objects accelerate because gravity is a force that pulls them downward. How can a pendulum's back-and-forth motion be used to measure the acceleration of falling objects?

EXPERIMENT 3.3

Springs, Forces, and Stretches

Question:

If you know how much a spring has been stretched by the force of a certain weight, can you predict how much it will stretch when more weight is added?

Hypothesis:

Yes, because the force that stretches the spring changes according to the amount of weight on the spring.

Materials:

- spring such as a screen-door spring or one from an old window shade
- pencil
- pliers
- meterstick
- clothespin
- standard masses (weights): 100 g to 1 kg
- graph paper
- a second but different spring
- scissors

Procedure:

1. Find a spring, such as one used to close screen doors or one you can remove from an old window shade. If necessary, use pliers to bend a loop at one end of the spring so that it can be hung from a hook or nail. Then bend a loop on the lower end of the spring so that weight can be hung from it.

Figure 19.

A spring stretches when a force pulls on it. How is the amount of stretch related to the force?

A one-kilogram weight hung from the spring should stretch it about one-quarter to one-third longer than its original length.

2. Fasten a meterstick near the spring, as shown in Figure 19. Then, with the meterstick in place, you can measure how much the spring will stretch when weights are hung on it. A clothespin can be used to mark the spring's very lowest point on the meterstick.

3. Now add masses to the spring. Measure and record the amount the spring stretches when each mass is hung from the spring.

   How much does the spring stretch when a 0.50-kg mass (500 g, which weighs 4.9 newtons) is carefully hung from it? (Newtons, symbolized with N, are discussed on page 54.) How much does it stretch when a 1.00-kg mass (9.8 N) is hung from the spring? Does doubling the force (weight) pulling on the spring double its stretch?

4. Predict the amount the spring will stretch when 1.50 kg (14.7 N) is hung on the spring. Predict the amount the spring will stretch when 0.25 kg (2.45 N) is hung on the spring. Test your predictions and record your measurements. Were your predictions correct?

5. Measure the amount the spring is stretched as you allow it to contract by removing masses.

Results and Conclusions

Are the values you find for stretch versus mass the same as they were when you were adding mass to the spring?

Using the data you have collected, plot a graph of the force on the spring, in newtons, versus the amount the spring is stretched, in meters (see Figure 20). Use the graph you have made to predict the amount the spring will be stretched when 100 g (0.98 N), 200 g (1.96 N), 750 g (7.35 N), and 1,200 g (11.76 N) are hung from the spring. Then test your predictions. Were they correct?

What can you conclude about the relationship between the force on a spring and the amount the spring is stretched? This relationship is known as Hooke's law. It's named for Robert Hooke, the seventeenth-century English scientist who first discovered it. The slope of the graph you have made, which has the units N/m, is called the spring constant.

Repeat the experiment with a different spring, such as one you can take from a spiral-bound notebook. With this smaller spring, you should probably use 1-newton to 5-newton (100-g to 500-g) weights. What is the spring constant for this second spring? What does the spring constant tell you about a spring's resistance to being stretched?

Do you think the spring constant will change if you change the spring's length? To find out, cut the notebook spring you used in half. What happens to the spring constant when you halve the length of the spring? Does it halve too? Does it double? Try to explain the results of this experiment.

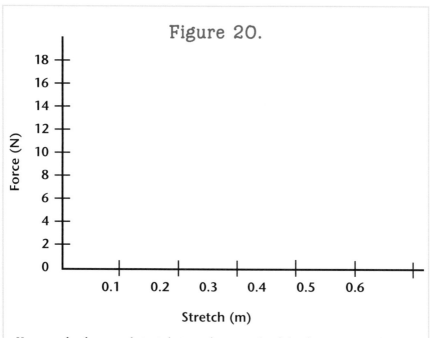

Figure 20.

Use axes for force and stretch to make a graph of the force on a spring versus the distance the spring stretches. The graph will enable you to find the spring constant.

 ## Science Project Ideas

- Repeat Experiment 3.3 using smaller masses and a long rubber band in place of the spring. Does a rubber band stretch according to Hooke's law?

- Using what you learned in Experiment 3.3, explain how a spring balance works. If the markings fell off a spring balance, how would you recalibrate it? How would the spring constants for a 10-N and a 1,000-N spring balance compare?

EXPERIMENT 3.4

Springs, Masses, and Time

Question:

Does the rise and fall of a spring pulled down by a weight have a fixed period?

Hypothesis:

Yes, but changing the amount of weight will change the period of the spring's rise and fall.

Materials:

- standard masses
- spring used in Experiment 3.3
- pencil
- meterstick
- stopwatch, or a watch that can measure seconds
- graph paper

Procedure:

1. Hang a 1.0-kg mass (weight) on the spring you first investigated in Experiment 3.3.

2. Lift the mass about 5 cm above its rest position and let it fall. As you can see, the weight rises and falls (oscillates) in a way that appears to have a fixed period, like a pendulum.

   Does this motion have a fixed period? Let's find out.

3. Use a stopwatch, or a watch that can measure seconds, to find the time for the mass to move down to its lowest position and back up again 10 times. Then measure the time for the mass to make 20 oscillations. Calculate the period for both 10 and 20 oscillations.

   Does the motion have a constant period? If it does, what is the period in seconds?

Results and Conclusions

You probably found that the mass of the bob doesn't affect the period of a pendulum. Does it affect the period of an oscillating spring? Let's find out.

Procedure:

1. Hang a 0.5-kg mass from the spring.

2. Measure and record the period of the oscillating spring. Has it changed? Does halving the mass halve the period?

   You know the period of the spring for masses of 1.0 kg and 0.5 kg. Now find the period of the oscillating spring for masses of 0.20 kg, 0.70 kg, 1.20 kg, and 1.5 kg as well.

3. Use the data you collect to plot a graph of the spring's period versus the mass suspended from the spring.

Results and Conclusions

Do your data points form a straight line? If not, try plotting the square of the period versus the mass.

Does doubling the mass double the square of the period? Does tripling the mass triple the square of the period? What do you find? What can you conclude?

Science Project Ideas

- Measure the length of an unstretched spring. Then hang masses from the spring until it's stretched to one-third longer than its original unstretched length. At this point, let the mass oscillate up and down. You'll find that after moving up and down a few times, the spring begins to swing like a pendulum. Then it returns to its up-and-down motion. What happens next? Have you seen anything like this before? Try to develop an explanation for this "undecided" spring's strange behavior.

- Repeat Experiment 3.4 using smaller masses and a long rubber band in place of the spring. Is the square of the period of oscillation of the rubber band doubled when the suspended mass doubles?

CHAPTER 4

Motions That Curve or Circle

The motions you investigated in the first three chapters of this book were along straight or slightly curved lines. In this chapter, you'll begin investigating the motion of objects that curve or even go in circles or ellipses, such as the satellites that orbit Earth.

According to Newton's second law of motion (see page 59), there must be a force to make an object change its velocity—that is, its direction or speed. A sideways force can cause an object to be pushed off a straight-line path and into a curved route. In the case of the slightly curved arc of a pendulum bob, you know that gravity causes the bob to fall. But what causes it to move along an arc rather than fall straight down? You'll investigate that question in Experiment 4.1.

◄ A satellite orbiting Earth travels in an elliptical path around the planet. Earth's gravity prevents the satellite from flying off into space.

EXPERIMENT 4.1

The Forces on a Pendulum Bob

Question:

Can you measure whether the downward force of a pendulum bob changes during each swing?

Hypothesis:

You can build a pendulum that measures when the force is greatest and least during each swing.

Materials:

- tape
- 0.2-kg (200-g) mass
- toy truck
- 5- or 10-newton (500-g or 1,000-g) spring scale
- board, 3–4 ft long
- wood blocks
- clamps
- strong string
- shelf or an elevated table or chair

Procedure:

1. Tape a 0.2-kg (200-g) mass to the body of a toy truck. Be sure the wheels are free to turn.

2. Suspend the mass and truck from a spring scale. With what force does gravity pull them straight downward?

3. Next, place the truck on an inclined plane, such as a board that has one end raised. Pull the truck and mass slowly up the incline. With what force does gravity pull the truck and mass down the incline?

Results and Conclusions

Gravity has been "diluted" by the incline. Less force is required to pull the objects along the incline than to lift them straight up. But that doesn't mean the objects weigh less.

Part of the weight is being pulled down along the incline—the part you pulled with the spring balance. The other part is pushing against the board (and the board is pushing back).

Procedure:

1. Now build a 1-m-long pendulum using the 0.2-kg mass as the bob (see Figure 21). Use clamps and wooden blocks to fasten the string to a shelf or an elevated table or chair.

2. Insert a 5- or 10-newton (500-g or 1,000-g) spring scale between the bob and the string as shown.

3. Pull the bob about 20 cm to one side. If the bob was not attached to the string, what would happen to it if you let go? With the string attached, what happens when you release it?

Results and Conclusions

Watch the spring scale as the bob swings back and forth. When is the force greatest? When is it least? What provides the force that keeps the bob from falling straight down? Why do you think the force on the bob changes as it swings?

Figure 21.

Build a pendulum with a spring scale inserted above the bob. When the pendulum swings, at what point is the force on the bob greatest? At what point is it least?

EXPERIMENT 4.2

Projectiles Launched Horizontally near Earth's Surface

Question:

If one object is dropped at the same time that a second object is hurled horizontally from the same height, which will land first?

Hypothesis:

Both will hit the ground at the same time.

Materials:

- 2 nickels
- table
- tape
- metal ball, diameter about 2 cm (¾ inch)
- clay
- meterstick
- carbon paper
- toy dart gun and plastic dart with suction cup
- large room or hallway
- carpenter's level
- large sheet of paper
- paper clip
- thread

An object fired or thrown into the air, such as a bullet or a baseball, is called a projectile. Once it leaves the gun, arm, or any device that projects it, the only forces acting on it are gravity and friction with the air, termed air resistance. Like any frictional force, air resistance will act against the motion of a projectile and reduce its speed. Gravity, of course, will pull the projectile downward. Gravity will cause it to fall off whatever path it has, whether horizontal or upward.

In outer space, beyond Earth's atmosphere, there is no air resistance. There the only force on satellites is gravity. It's gravity that causes these satellites to follow curved paths (orbits) around Earth.

It was Galileo who, after watching cannonballs in flight, first realized that vertical and horizontal motions are independent of one another. If one object is dropped at the same time that a second object is hurled horizontally from the same height, both will hit the ground at the same time.

Procedure:

1. To see that this is true, place a nickel at the edge of a table. Place a second nickel a short distance behind the first one, as shown in Figure 22.

2. Snap your finger against the second nickel so that it strikes the first one.

   The first nickel will fly off horizontally and land some distance from the table. The second will fall almost vertically to the floor. Listen carefully! Do the coins strike the floor at the same or at different times? What can you conclude about the vertical acceleration of the two coins?

   It takes 0.45 second for an object to fall 1.0 meter. You can use this information to measure the horizontal velocity of a weighted dart.

Figure 22.

If one coin falls straight to the floor while the other flies off horizontally, will the two coins land at the same time?

3. Tape a metal ball with a diameter of about 2 cm ($\frac{3}{4}$ inch) to the suction cup of a plastic dart that can be fired from a toy dart gun.

4. Place the toy gun on a table. Use clay to hold it in place horizontally at exactly 1.0 meter (39 $\frac{3}{8}$ inches) above a long stretch of horizontal floor. A carpenter's level can be used to make sure the toy pistol is aimed horizontally.

5. Put the weighted dart in the gun. **Safety:** *Be sure no one is in front of the toy pistol.* Pull the trigger and watch to see where the dart lands.

6. To mark its landing point more accurately, place a large sheet of white paper in the vicinity where you saw the dart strike the floor. Place a sheet of carbon paper on the white paper so that the dart will leave a mark when it lands.

7. To find the horizontal distance the dart traveled, make a plumb line (a weight attached to a line) by tying a paper clip or other weight to a piece of thread.

8. Place the upper end of the thread against the end of the weighted dart in the pistol. The weight at the lower end will lie directly under the end of the dart, making a vertical line to the floor.

9. Measure the distance from the lower end of the plumb line to the point where the dart landed. This is the horizontal distance the dart traveled.

Results and Conclusions

What was the horizontal velocity of the weighted dart? Use the graph in Figure 23 to find the vertical velocity of the dart when it struck the floor.

How do you think the horizontal velocity of the unweighted dart will compare with that of the weighted dart? Find a room large enough to allow the unweighted dart to strike the floor. **Safety:** *Again, be sure no one is in front of the toy pistol.* Fire the unweighted dart and find its horizontal velocity.

Figure 23.

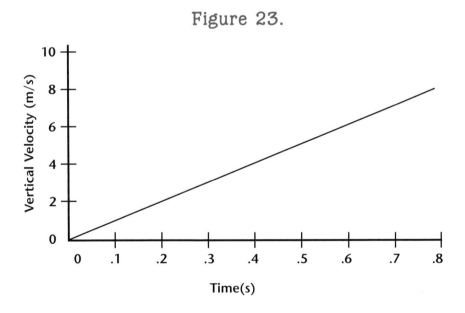

The graph shows the vertical velocity of a falling object versus time. What does the graph indicate about the object's acceleration? What is the acceleration in m/s/s?

Science Project Ideas

- Design another way to show that an object projected horizontally falls with the same acceleration as one that falls straight down.

- Use the data from your experiment and the graph in Figure 23 to make a scaled map of the path followed by the weighted dart projectile.

EXPERIMENT 4.3

Your Bike and a Water Balloon Projectile

Question:

If you drop a water balloon from a moving bike, will the balloon go straight down?

Hypothesis:

No, it will also have horizontal movement.

Materials:

- chalk or flour
- level sidewalk or path
- water
- balloons
- bicycle
- bicycle helmet
- tape measure

Procedure:

1. Use some chalk or flour to make a target at one side of a level sidewalk or path.

2. Next, make a few water balloons and seal them by tying the necks.

3. **Safety:** *Be sure the path is clear. Fasten your bike helmet.* Hold the balloon against your bike's handlebar and ride toward the target. When the balloon is directly above the target, release it.

Did the water balloon hit the target? If not, where did it land? Why do you think it did not hit the target?

4. Repeat the experiment while riding your bike at different speeds. How does the speed at which your bike is traveling change the horizontal distance the balloon travels before it hits the ground?

5. Repeat the experiment, but this time release the water balloon at a point that you think will cause it to strike the target. How close did you come?

Results and Conclusions

If you know the height, in meters, through which an object falls, the time for it to fall is approximately the square root of two-tenths the height. That is,

$$\text{time to fall} = \sqrt{0.2h}$$

How can you use this information, together with measurements you can make, to find the speed of your bike when you drop the water balloon?

EXPERIMENT 4.4

Projectiles Launched at Upward Angles Near Earth's Surface

Question:

Can you find out whether the angle at which something is launched affects how far it travels horizontally?

Hypothesis:

By measuring the distances traveled by several toy darts fired at different angles, you can see how angle of launch affects distance.

Materials:

- toy dart gun and weighted dart used in Experiment 4.2
- sheet of cardboard
- protractor
- ruler
- pen or pencil
- paper
- carbon paper
- water hose and nozzle

Most projectiles are launched at an angle above the horizon. You can use the toy dart gun and weighted dart you used in Experiment 4.2 to measure the range (horizontal distance traveled) of projectiles fired at different angles.

Figure 24.

An enlarged protractor can be used to launch a weighted dart at different angles. Which angle gives the greatest range?

Procedure:

1. Make a large half protractor, like the one shown in Figure 24, from a sheet of cardboard. Simply extend the lines of an ordinary protractor to make the larger version.

2. **Safety:** *Make sure no one is in front of the toy pistol!* Fire the weighted dart at different angles, making certain that the dart is always the same distance above the floor. Use paper and carbon paper to mark the landing points.

Results and Conclusions

For which angle or angles does the dart travel farthest horizontally?

In warm weather, you can repeat this experiment using a water hose with a nozzle that allows you to make a fast narrow stream. Does the greatest range for the hose occur at the same angle as for the toy gun?

EXPERIMENT 4.5

Circular Motion, Newton, and Forces

Question:

How can you observe the force that makes objects travel in a circle?

Hypothesis:

You can observe that force when you swing an object in a circle.

Materials:

- plastic pail
- water
- measuring cup
- 20-newton (2,000-g) spring scale
- a friend
- short, thin rope
- vial or test-tube accelerometer from Experiment 2.3
- turntable or Lazy Susan

Newton's first law tells us that an object will maintain its velocity along a *straight* line unless acted upon by a force. From this law, we can assume that there must be a force on any object that follows a circular path. If there were no such force, the object would move along a straight line. If an object is following a circular path at constant speed, there can be no force pushing it along the circle. If there were, the object would accelerate; its speed would increase or decrease. Therefore, the force making the object move in a circle must be perpendicular to the motion, along the radii of the circle.

Procedure:

1. To see that this is true, half fill a plastic pail with water.

2. **Safety:** *Take the pail outside where there is no danger of the pail hitting anything or anyone.* Grasp the pail with both hands and swing it in a horizontal circle as you turn in place.

Results and Conclusions:

Notice that you have to pull inward to make the pail move in a circle. At the same time, you feel a force pulling your arms outward. This outward pull is what you would expect according to Newton's third law—for every action there is an equal and opposite reaction.

The inward force on the pail is called a centripetal force. The outward force on you is called a centrifugal force.

You can measure the force needed to move an object along a circular path.

Procedure:

1. Pour one cup (250 mL) of water into the plastic pail.

2. Attach a 20-N (2,000-g) spring scale to the pail.

3. Hold on to the spring scale with both hands as you turn in place, swinging the pail in a horizontal circle at a constant speed.

4. Ask a friend to tell you if your speed is constant. With what force do you pull inward on the pail? With what outward force does the pail pull on you?

Do you think the force will increase, decrease, or stay the same if you increase the speed at which the pail moves in a circle of the same radius? Try it! Were you correct?

Do you think the force will increase, decrease, or remain the same if you increase the radius of the circle through which the pail moves?

5. First measure the force on the pail when you move it in a circle at the same rate of turning as before.

6. Then tie one end of a short, thin rope to the pail's handle. Tie the other end to the spring scale.

7. Now move the pail along the larger circular path while you turn at the same rate as before.

Results and Conclusions

What do you find? Does the force change when the radius of the circular path changes? If it does, does it increase or decrease as the radius gets bigger?

If you have ever ridden a loop-the-loop roller coaster, you may have wondered why you did not fall out when you were upside down. The answer is really quite simple. The centripetal force is greater than the force due to gravity. You'll feel the roller coaster seat pushing against you even at the top of the loop. The seat is accelerating toward the center of the circle at a greater rate than if gravity were making it fall toward the ground.

You can do a loop-the-loop with your pail of water. **Safety:** *But be sure you're outdoors.* Instead of swinging the pail in a horizontal circle, swing it in a vertical circle. Does the water stay in the pail when it's upside down? How does the centripetal force on the water compare with the gravitational force on it?

Centripetal Acceleration

According to Newton's second law, objects experiencing a centripetal force must also experience a centripetal acceleration.

Procedure:

1. To test this conclusion, tape a vial or test-tube accelerometer to a turntable or Lazy Susan. (See Experiment 2.3.)

2. Be sure the accelerometer is level so that the bubble is in the center of the tube.

3. Start the turntable or spin the Lazy Susan.

Results and Conclusions

What does the accelerometer indicate about the direction of the acceleration? Does it confirm the conclusion based on Newton's second law?

Use what you learned from your experiment with the pail and spring scale to predict the answer to the following questions. Then do the experiments needed to confirm your answers. What will happen to the acceleration if you increase the speed at which the turntable or Lazy Susan spins? What will happen to the acceleration if you decrease the speed at which the table turns? What will happen to the acceleration if you move the accelerometer closer to the center of the turntable or Lazy Susan? What will happen to the acceleration if you move the accelerometer farther from the center of the turntable or Lazy Susan? Where can you place the accelerometer so that there will be no acceleration?

 ## Science Project Ideas

- **Ask an adult** to accompany you on a visit to an amusement park and enjoy the many rides. On how many of those rides does a centripetal force act on you?

- Take an accelerometer to a playground. Explain what you observe as you watch the accelerometer on a whirl-around and on a swing as you move a short distance to and fro.

EXPERIMENT 4.6

A Circling Satellite

Question:

What would happen to Earth's satellites if the force of gravity were turned off?

Hypothesis:

They would fly into deep space.

Materials:

- marble or steel ball
- large plastic lid
- scissors

A satellite in orbit about Earth is constantly pulled inward by a force. The inward-acting force is gravity, which pulls the satellite toward Earth's center. Of course, according to Newton's third law of motion, the satellite exerts an equal but opposite force on Earth. However, the force has little effect on Earth's motion because Earth has so much more mass than satellites— except for one particular satellite, that is. The one exception is the moon, our largest satellite, which is massive enough to affect Earth's motion.

A simple experiment can demonstrate what would happen to satellites, including the moon, if the force of gravity could suddenly be turned off.

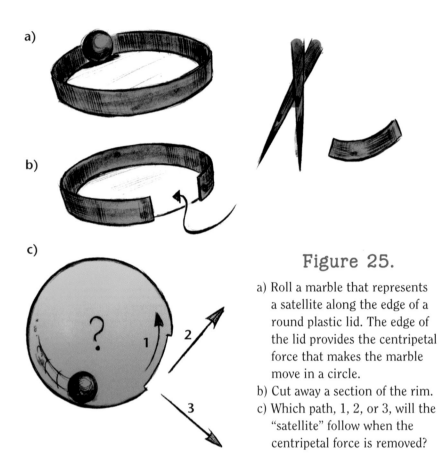

a)

b)

c)

Figure 25.

a) Roll a marble that represents a satellite along the edge of a round plastic lid. The edge of the lid provides the centripetal force that makes the marble move in a circle.

b) Cut away a section of the rim.

c) Which path, 1, 2, or 3, will the "satellite" follow when the centripetal force is removed?

Procedure:

1. Place a marble or steel ball inside the rim of a large circular plastic lid resting on a table or counter as shown in Figure 25a. The lid should be an extra one that can be destroyed.

2. Give the ball a push and watch it follow a circular path around the outside edge of the lid.

   In this experiment, the rolling marble or ball represents a satellite. The outside wall of the lid supplies the inward push, the "gravity" that keeps the ball moving in a circle.

What do you think will happen if the centripetal force is suddenly removed?

3. Use scissors to cut away a small section of the plastic lid's rim (Figure 25b).

4. If you now start the marble or ball rolling around the edge, which of the paths shown in Figure 25c do you think the sphere will follow? Try it! Were you right?

Results and Conclusions

See if you can explain why it takes the path it does. Why do satellites not fly off into deep space and out of the solar system?

EXPERIMENT 4.7

Weightlessness on an Orbiting Satellite or Spaceship

Question:

Can you observe weightlessness in everyday situations?

Hypothesis:

Yes. You can study weightlessness by observing how the force of gravity changes during free-falls.

Materials:

- nail
- Styrofoam cups
- water
- 2 rubber bands
- paper clip
- tape
- 2 metal washers
- 1-kg or similar mass
- 20-newton (2,000-g) spring scale
- pillows
- elevator
- bathroom scale

It was Sir Isaac Newton who first recognized the possibility of sending human-made satellites into orbit. Newton calculated that an object launched horizontally from a point above Earth's atmosphere at a speed of about 28,000 kph (17,500 mph) would orbit Earth. The force of gravity would provide the centripetal force needed for the satellite to circle Earth.

Since gravity pulls the satellite downward, it would fall toward Earth just as would a football thrown horizontally. However, because the satellite is moving so fast, Earth curves away from it at the same rate that it falls (see Figure 26).

Suppose you were aboard one of NASA's space shuttles or the International Space Station in orbit around Earth. Both you and the space-ship would be falling toward Earth. Unless you grabbed something and pushed or pulled yourself, you would float about inside the ship. You would feel weightless. Your feet might be touching the floor of the ship, but it wouldn't be like standing on Earth. You wouldn't feel any pressure on your feet because the ship would be falling out from under you. It would be like

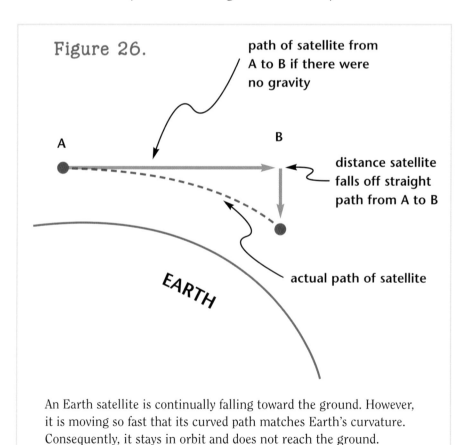

Figure 26.

path of satellite from A to B if there were no gravity

A

B

distance satellite falls off straight path from A to B

EARTH

actual path of satellite

An Earth satellite is continually falling toward the ground. However, it is moving so fast that its curved path matches Earth's curvature. Consequently, it stays in orbit and does not reach the ground.

riding in a free-falling elevator. You would have a prolonged sensation of what you feel when you fall back to Earth after jumping as high as you can.

Under weightless conditions, many things behave strangely. For example, water will not flow from a tap. You can do simple experiments to demonstrate this.

Procedure:

1. Use a nail to make two holes on opposite sides near the bottom of a Styrofoam cup, as shown in Figure 27a.

2. Take the cup outside, put your fingers over the holes, and fill the cup with water.

3. Hold the cup as high above the ground as possible. Then release the cup. What happens to the water streams as the cup falls? How can you explain what you observe?

4. Another approach is to slip two rubber bands through a hole in the bottom of a Styrofoam cup. The rubber bands must be long enough to hang over the top of the cup. A paper clip attached to the ends of the rubber bands below the cup will prevent them from sliding through the hole (see Figure 27b).

5. To the other ends of the rubber bands, which hang over opposite sides of the cup, tape metal washers.

6. Hold the cup out at arm's length and release it.

Results and Conclusions

What happens to the washers when they become weightless? How can you explain what you observe?

What do you think you would find if you tried to weigh yourself in a spaceship orbiting Earth?

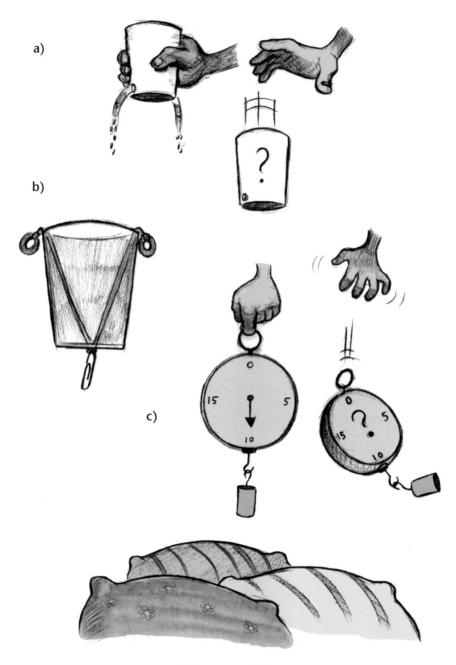

Figure 27.

a) What happens to water flow under weightless conditions?
b) What happens to the washers when they are weightless?
c) What happens to the weight reading on the spring scale under weightless conditions?

Procedure:

1. Hang a one-kg mass from a 20-N spring scale, as shown in Figure 27c. What is the weight of the kilogram mass in newtons?

2. Place some pillows on the floor.

3. Hold the spring balance and the suspended one-kg mass as high above the pillows as possible. Then release the spring balance.

Results and Conclusions

What is the reading on the spring balance as it falls? How can you explain what you observe?

You can see the effect of partial weightlessness in an elevator. Stand on a bathroom scale when the elevator is at rest. What is your weight? Press the button for a lower floor. Watch closely as the elevator accelerates downward. What happens to your weight as recorded on the scale? How can you explain what you observe?

Predict what will happen if you repeat the experiment but push the button for a higher floor. Try it! Were you right?

 ## Science Project Ideas

- Astronauts on the International Space Station are able to determine their mass. How can they do this if they are weightless? Build a balance that could be used to measure mass under weightless conditions.

- Describe what must be done in order to eat, sleep, and perform other life functions under conditions of weightlessness.

CHAPTER 5

Forces, Machines, and Muscles

Compared with other animals, the physical abilities of humans are not outstanding. Many animals can run much faster than we; many have greater strength, better vision, better hearing, and a keener sense of smell. It's intellect, the ability to think, communicate, and reason, that is the great human advantage. Intellect has enabled us to build machines that can provide forces far exceeding the strength of any animal; to construct vehicles that can move faster than Earth turns; to construct devices that can see deep into the universe or detect sounds below the hearing threshold of any animal.

Over the course of history, humans have developed six simple machines, as well as many complex ones.

◀ Pumpjacks dot the landscape in oil-rich areas. These machines are used to force oil out of the well.

The simple machines are the lever, inclined plane, pulley, wheel and axle, wedge, and screw. Some of these machines help humans produce forces far stronger than our muscles can. Others have made the motions involved in work far easier to accomplish.

In this chapter you'll explore simple machines that can change the effect or direction of forces. You'll also see how human muscles and bones are related to machines and how humans use machines to make work easier.

EXPERIMENT 5.1

The Lever: A Simple Machine

Question:

How can a lever make work easier?

Hypothesis:

The length of a lever is related to the amount of force needed to lift an object.

Materials:

- 30-cm (1-ft) wooden ruler
- pencil
- book
- plastic soda straw
- long pin
- 2 identical cans
- felt-tipped pen
- paper clips
- a friend
- clay

Procedure:

1. Place a 30-cm (1-ft) wooden ruler on a pencil. The ruler will serve as a lever. The pencil is the fulcrum, the position about which the lever turns. At what position will the ruler balance (not tip to one side) on the pencil?

2. When the ruler is balanced, place a book at one end of the ruler. Use your hand to prevent the book from falling, but don't push the book either up or down.

3. Lift the book by pushing on the other end of the ruler. Get a sense of the force needed to lift the book.

4. Now move the pencil (fulcrum) close to the book, as shown in Figure 28. Again, sense the force needed for you to lift the book.

What has happened to the force you need to apply to lift the book?

Figure 28.

A ruler can act as a lever, with a pencil serving as a fulcrum.

Results and Conclusions

What do you think will be true of the force you need to apply to lift the book if you move the fulcrum farther from the book? Try it! Were you right? Are there places you can put the fulcrum under the ruler so that you can't lift the book? If there are, where are they?

How can a lever be used to make work easier? How can it be used to make work harder? Let's find out.

Procedure:

1. Use a soda straw and a long pin to make an equal-arm lever.

2. Measure with a ruler to find the exact middle of the straw. Push the pin through the middle of the straw and slightly above the center, as shown in Figure 29a.

3. Place the ends of the pin on two identical cans as shown. To see why the pin was inserted above the center, simply turn the straw over so that the pin lies below the straw's center.

   The pin will serve as a fulcrum for your equal-arm lever. Why is it called an equal-arm lever?

4. Use a felt-tipped pen to make marks 3 cm, 6 cm, and 9 cm from the pin on both sides of the straw, as shown in Figure 29b.

5. Hang a paper clip 9 cm from the pin on one side of the balanced straw. (If the clip slides on the straw, bend it together enough to make it stay in place.)

   Assuming that all your paper clips have the same weight, where should you place a paper clip on the other side of the straw to make it balance? Where can you place three paper clips on the other side of the straw lever to make it balance?

Results and Conclusions

The drawings in Figure 29c show some arrangements of paper clips on the left side of the straw balance. For each case shown, how can you add one or more paper clips to the right side of the straw to balance it? In some cases, is there more than one way to make it balance? For example,

Figure 29.

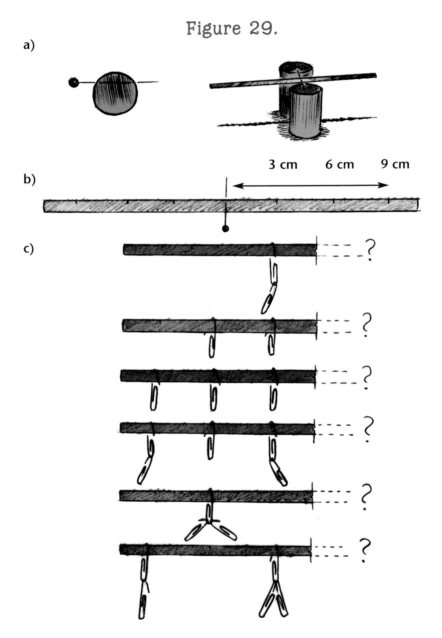

a) The pin should be above the center of the straw.

b) Make marks 3 cm, 6 cm, and 9 cm from the midpoint of the straw.

c) Using paper clips on the other side of the lever, how can each of these straws be balanced?

in how many of the cases shown can you balance the straw by using just one paper clip on the right side? Two paper clips on the right side? Three paper clips? Four? More than four?

Continue to experiment with your soda straw balance, using paper clips on each side. Can you discover a rule (law) that enables you to predict ways to balance the straw lever?

Once you think you have discovered the law of the lever, ask a friend to set up the left side of the balance with paper clips. Then predict the various ways you can make the beam balance. Test your predictions. Does your law always work?

Next, experiment with an unequal-arm lever.

Procedure:

1. Move the support pin (fulcrum) 3 cm to the left of the center position to make an unequal-arm lever, as shown in Figure 30a. The straw will not balance now because more of its weight is to the right of the fulcrum.

2. Add a small piece of clay to the left of the fulcrum to make the straw balance.

Results and Conclusions

Which of the arrangements in Figure 30b will balance? Continue to test the unequal-arm lever with different combinations of weights to see if your lever law still holds true. What do you find?

The distance from the fulcrum to the force or weight on the lever is called the lever arm. The lever arm times the force is called the moment of force. In the experiments you have just done, the moments of force on

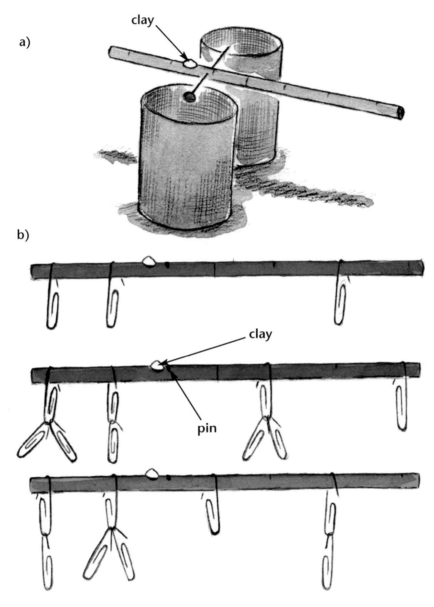

Figure 30.

a) Make an unequal-arm lever by moving the pin 3 cm to the left of the pin's middle. Does your law of the lever still hold true?

b) Which of the levers shown here will be balanced?

the right side of the lever tended to turn the lever clockwise. The moments of force on the left side of the lever tended to turn the lever counterclockwise. A paper clip may be considered one unit of weight.

For each balanced lever, how did the clockwise moment or moments of force compare with the counterclockwise moment or moments of force?

 ## Science Project Ideas

- There are three classes of levers. Find out how levers are classified and find examples of each in simple machines such as wheelbarrows, crowbars, pulleys, hammers, and shovels.

- You use simple levers every time you eat with a knife, fork, and spoon. Make a list of the levers you see every day. Then identify them as first-, second-, or third-class levers.

- Levers can be used to provide a mechanical advantage. What is meant by *mechanical advantage*? How can a lever provide a mechanical advantage? Can a mechanical advantage ever be less than 1?

EXPERIMENT 5.2

The Lever as a Sensitive Balance

Question:

Can a lever be used to show differences in the weight of very small objects?

Hypothesis:

A lever can be used as part of a sensitive balance, which will allow you to weigh very small things.

Materials:

- small machine screw that can be inserted into the end of a plastic soda straw
- plastic soda straw
- pin
- scissors
- 2 glass microscope slides
- small wood block
- rubber band
- graph paper
- laboratory balance
- clothespin
- index card
- pen or pencil
- sand

Procedure:

1. To begin, push a small machine screw about halfway into one end of a plastic soda straw.

2. Use scissors to cut out a small piece from the top of the straw on the end opposite the machine screw. The cutout area will serve as a small balance pan.

3. Balance the straw and the screw on your finger. Push a pin through the straw at the balance point. Be sure the pin, which will serve as the fulcrum, is just above the vertical midpoint of the straw, as shown in Figures 29, 30, and 31.

Figure 31.

rubber band

A sensitive balance can be made from simple materials.

4. Place the fulcrum pin on a pair of glass microscope slides fastened to a small block with a rubber band, as shown in Figure 31.

5. Turn the machine screw, moving it into or out of the straw, until the straw tilts up at approximately 30 degrees.

6. To calibrate your balance, first find the mass, in grams, of a sheet of graph paper on a laboratory balance. Next, calculate the mass of one small square of the paper. For example, if the sheet weighs 3.0 g and contains 900 squares, each square must weigh 3.0 g ÷ 900, or 0.0033 g.

7. A clothespin can be used to support an index card next to the balance pan. Use a pen or pencil to mark the position of the pan on the card. Then place a known mass of paper squares on the pan. (In the example given, three squares would equal 0.01 g.)

8. Mark the new level of the pan on the card. Write the corresponding mass beside the mark. Do the same for several known masses.

Results and Conclusions

What range of masses can you weigh with this balance? Can you weigh a grain of sand? What is good about this balance? What are its limitations?

Science Project Ideas

- Try to build a balance as sensitive as the one you made in Experiment 5.2 but with fewer limitations than that balance has.

- Do you think you weigh more standing up or lying down? Or do you think you weigh the same either way? To find out, place a board about as long as you are tall on a bathroom scale. Have someone record the weight of you plus the board when you lie on the board. Then find your weight when you stand on the board. What do you conclude?

- What is your weight when it's recorded on two bathroom scales? Put one end of a board on one scale and the other end on a second scale. Have a partner record the readings on both scales when you stand at different places on the board. What do you find? Are the results different if you move the scales to different places under the board?

- Mobiles are a form of art based on levers. Use wires, thread, and various small objects to build mobiles. Let your imagination and the lever principle you have discovered serve as guides.

 EXPERIMENT 5.3

The Inclined Plane and Work

Question:

Do simple machines affect the amount of force needed to do physical work?

Hypothesis:

Yes, simple machines, such as an inclined plane, reduce the amount of force needed to do work.

Materials:

- tape
- 0.2-kg mass
- toy truck
- long board
- books
- 5- or 10-newton (500-g or 1,000-g) spring scale
- meterstick or metric ruler

Scientists define *work* as the product of force and the distance through which the force acts. If you exert a force of 10 newtons to lift a weight through a height of 2 meters, you do 20 newton-meters (N-m) of work because 10 N × 2 m = 20 N-m.

Sometimes it makes sense to use a machine to reduce the force even though you may do more work. To see why, try the following experiment.

Procedure:

1. Tape a 0.2-kg mass to a toy truck. Use a 5- or 10-newton (500-g or 1,000-g) spring scale to weigh the truck and mass.

2. Use a long board and some books to build an inclined plane like the one you built in Chapter 4. What is the distance from the floor to the high end of the inclined plane? How much work would you do if you lifted the loaded truck from the floor straight up to the top of the incline?

3. Place the loaded truck at the low end of the incline.

Results and Conclusions

What force is needed to pull the truck slowly up the inclined plane? How much less force is needed to pull the truck along the incline than to lift it straight up? What is the advantage of using an inclined plane?

What is the length of the inclined plane? How much work is required to move the truck along the full length of the inclined plane? Why might this work be more than the work required to lift the truck straight up? Why might you use an inclined plane to raise a heavy load even if it involved more work?

 Science Project Ideas

- How many examples can you find in which inclined planes are being used to make work easier? If possible, determine how much the force is reduced by using the inclined plane and how much work is done using the simple machine. How does the angle of the incline affect the force needed to move an object up the incline? How does it affect the work done?

- Use a lever to lift a heavy weight. How does the force you exert compare with the weight lifted? How does the work you put in compare with the work output— the work done on the weight?

EXPERIMENT 5.4

Work and the Pulley

Question:

Why are pulleys used to lift objects?

Hypothesis:

Pulleys reduce the amount of force needed to do the lifting.

Materials:

- 3 pulleys or 2 wood dowels or smooth, rigid cardboard tubes
- hook
- 2 friends
- measuring cup
- water
- plastic pail
- 20-newton (2,000-g) spring scale
- strong string

Procedure:

1. Pulleys are one of the six simple machines. If you have a pulley, fasten it to a hook as shown in Figure 32a. If you don't have a pulley, substitute a wood dowel or a smooth, rigid cardboard tube and have someone hold it firmly against a counter or tabletop.

a)

b)

Figure 32.

Using pulleys to do work.

2. Pour about a liter (quart) of water into a plastic pail.

3. Use a 20-newton (2,000-g) spring scale to weigh the pail of water.

4. Now lift the pail using strong string and the pulley, dowel, or tube as shown. With what force do you have to pull downward to raise the pail?

Why would anyone use a pulley to lift a weight? (Remember, a machine can be used to change the direction as well as the size of a force.) Next, lift the pail a different way.

5. Use three pulleys or two dowels or rigid cardboard tubes with the string wrapped a number of times around the dowels or tubes, as shown in Figure 32b. If you use dowels or tubes, a person will be needed to support the dowel next to the pail. That person shouldn't exert a force. He or she should simply keep the dowel or tube in a horizontal position.

Results and Conclusions

How does the force needed to lift the pail now compare with the weight of the pail? Investigate how the number of strings pulling upward on the pail affects the force needed to lift the pail. What do you find?

EXPERIMENT 5.5

Muscles and Bones as Levers

Question:

Can human muscles and bones be considered forms of levers?

Hypothesis:

The bones act as levers while the muscles apply the force needed to move them and accomplish work.

Materials:

- bathroom scale
- heavy table or counter
- chair
- small block of wood
- cloth

Figure 33a shows how the human arm serves as a third-class lever. (Figure 33b shows a first-class lever and a second-class lever.) The elbow serves as the fulcrum. The biceps and brachialis muscles, attached to the bones of the lower arm, pull upward. Their upward force allows the arm to lift weights in the hand.

You have done experiments with levers and you know about moments of force. Based on your knowledge and the experiments you have done, do you think you could lift more with your fingers, your wrist, or your forearm?

To find out, carry out the following experiment.

Procedure:

1. Place a bathroom scale against the underside of a heavy table or counter. Let the dial extend out far enough so that you can see it.

2. Sit in front of the scale with your arm at a right angle when in contact with the scale, as shown in Figure 34. (Sit on pillows if necessary.)

3. Wrap a small block of wood in some cloth. Use the block to push against the scale. Using your fingertips, with how much force can you push upward? With your wrist? With your forearm?

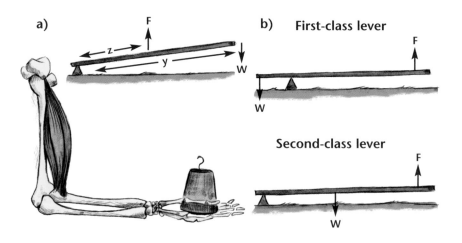

Figure 33.

a) The human arm works like a third-class lever. The elbow is the fulcrum. The biceps and brachialis muscles pull upward on the bones of the lower arm (radius and ulna), providing a counterclockwise moment of force, $F \times z$. The clockwise moment of force, $W \times y$, is produced by the weight in the hand.

b) First- and second-class levers. Levers are classified according to the relative position of fulcrum, force applied (F), and weight lifted.

Figure 34.

Can you lift more
with your fingertips,
wrist, or forearm?

Results and Conclusions

Explain your results based on your knowledge of levers. Do the results of
this experiment agree with your predictions?

 Science Project Ideas

- What other examples of muscles acting as levers can
  you find in your body? Are they all third-class levers?

- Find examples of second- and third-class levers that
  are in common use.

EXPERIMENT 5.6

Arm Versus Leg Strength

Question:

Which do you think are stronger levers, your arms or your legs?

Hypothesis:

By lifting different amounts of weights with your arms and legs, you can determine which are stronger levers.

Materials:

- weight room **with an adult trainer**
- notebook
- pen or pencil

To find out whether legs or arms are stronger, go to a weight room.

Procedure:

1. **Under the guidance of an adult trainer**, measure the strength of the muscles of your arm that cause your arm to bend. How much weight can you lift upward using your arm as shown in Figure 35a?

2. How much can you lift with the muscles that cause your leg to bend (Figure 35b)? Record your results. Which are stronger, the muscles that bend your arm or your leg?

3. Now measure the strength of the arm and leg muscles that you use to straighten your arm or leg (see Figures 35c and 35d). Record your results.

Results and Conclusions

Which are stronger, the muscles that straighten your arm or those that straighten your leg? Save your results. You'll need them for the next experiment.

a)

b)

c)

d)

Figure 35.

Which are stronger, the muscles of your arms or legs?

EXPERIMENT 5.7

Muscle Pairs

Question:

How can you measure which leg muscles are stronger, flexor or extender?

Hypothesis:

Simply exerting pressure against a bathroom scale will show muscle strength.

Materials:

- a wall
- bathroom scale
- a friend
- chair

In Experiment 5.6 you measured the strength of the muscles that cause your arms and legs to bend. Muscles that cause joints such as the knee and elbow to bend are called flexors. Muscles that straighten joints are called extensors.

As you saw in Experiment 5.6, muscles are paired. They must be paired because muscles can move joints only by pulling on bones; they can't push on them. An action produced by one muscle or set of muscles is opposed by another muscle or set of muscles. Were the muscles that caused your leg to bend (flex) stronger, weaker, or equal in strength to the muscles that caused your leg to straighten (extend)? Were the flexor muscles of your arm stronger, weaker, or equal in strength to the muscles that caused extension of your arm?

In many muscle pairs, one is often stronger than the other. A bathroom scale can be used to compare the strengths of some other muscle pairs. Compare the strength of the opposing muscles that allow you to kick a ball forward or backward.

Procedure:

1. Stand facing a wall. Put the scale upright against the wall. Have a friend hold the scale in place. With what force can you push your toe forward against the scale?

2. Next, put the scale between your heel and the leg of the chair. Again, have a friend hold the scale in place. With what force can you push backward with your heel?

Results and Conclusions

Are the muscles of this pair equal in strength? Arrange the scale so that you can compare other muscle pairs for strength. For example, compare the strengths of the muscle pairs used to 1) turn your toes upward or downward; 2) flex or extend your fingers; 3) move your head forward or backward; 4) move your head to the right or to the left; 5) move your upper arm forward or backward. What is the reason for the results you have from this experiment?

 Science Project Ideas

- Design and carry out an experiment to see how fatigue affects the strength of a muscle pair. Does it affect the strength of one member of a pair more than the other?

- Design and conduct another experiment to find out whether fatigue affects your ability to control a muscle.

EXPERIMENT 5.8

The Body's Center of Mass

Question:

When your body is balanced on a fulcrum, where is your center of mass positioned?

Hypothesis:

Your center of mass will be directly above the fulcrum.

Materials:

- meterstick
- a wall
- full-length mirror
- padded sawhorse or sofa with a soft arm
- a friend
- long, strong, uniform board
- bathroom scale
- narrow flat stick
- thick board
- tape measure

The center of mass of any object is the point where all its mass can be considered to be located. It's also the object's balance point—the point about which the moments of force causing it to rotate in opposite directions are equal.

The center of mass of some objects is easily located. For example, the center of mass of a sphere, such as a ball, is at its center. The center of mass of a meterstick is at the 50-cm mark.

Procedure:

1. Put your finger under the 50-cm mark of a meterstick. Does the stick balance on your finger? What happens if you put your finger under the 40-cm mark? Why do you think it happens? Like everything else, your body has a center of mass. For most people, it's located a few inches below the belly button (navel). What will happen if your center of mass is not above your body's points of support (your feet)?

2. Stand with your right leg and shoulder firmly against a wall. What happens when you lift your left foot? Normally, your body automatically adjusts so as to keep your center of mass above a point of support.

3. To see one way this is done, stand in front of a full-length mirror. Raise your left foot off the floor. How does your body adjust so that your center of mass is above your right foot? What happens if you lift your right foot instead of your left?

4. You can find the approximate location of your center of mass by lying rigidly on a padded sawhorse or the soft arm of a sofa (see Figure 36a). Either can serve as a fulcrum for your body, which you can think of as a lever. When your body is balanced, your center of mass will be directly above the fulcrum. Try it! What is the approximate location of your center of mass?

5. To find your center of mass more accurately, you'll need a long, strong, uniform board, a fulcrum, and a bathroom scale. Weigh the board by placing it on the bathroom scale.

6. Next, weigh a friend in the same way. Then place one end of the board on the center of the bathroom scale. Put the other end on a narrow flat stick resting on a thick board. The stick will serve as a fulcrum.

7. Ask your friend to lie on the board with the bottoms of his feet over the fulcrum as shown in Figure 36b. You now have a second-class lever.

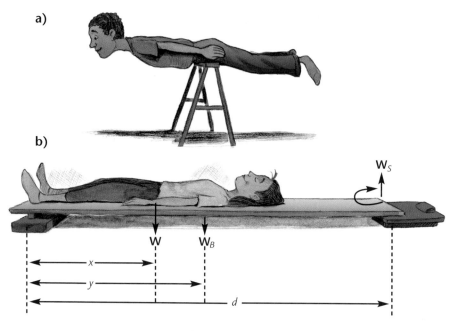

Figure 36.

a) You can make a rough determination of the location of your center of mass by balancing your body on a sawhorse.

b) You can more accurately find your center of mass by calculating moments of force.

Results and Conclusions

Your friend's entire weight, W, can be considered to be at his center of mass. The board's weight, W_B, and its center of mass will be at the center of the board. The distance from the fulcrum to the board's center of mass is represented by y; the distance from the fulcrum to your friend's center of mass is represented by x, which is unknown initially. The weights of your friend and the board create clockwise moments of force about the fulcrum. They are shown as $W \times x$ and $W_B \times y$ in Figure 36b.

The counterclockwise moment of force is the product of the force shown on the bathroom scale, W_S, and the distance from the fulcrum, d; that is, $W_S \times d$.

Since there is no rotation, the clockwise moments must equal the counterclockwise moments. Consequently,

$$(W \times x) + (W_B \times y) = (W_S \times d)$$

Suppose the board is 7 feet long (from the fulcrum to the scale) and weighs 10 pounds, and your friend weighs 100 pounds. The board's center of mass will be 3.5 feet from the fulcrum. If the scale reads 40 pounds, then:

$$(100 \text{ lb} \times x) + (10 \text{ lb} \times 3.5 \text{ ft}) = 40 \text{ lb} \times 7 \text{ ft}$$

$$100 \text{ lb} \times x + 35 \text{ lb-ft} = 280 \text{ lb-ft}$$

If you subtract 35 lb-ft from both sides of the equation, you have:

$$100 \text{ lb} \times x = 280 \text{ lb-ft} - 35 \text{ lb-ft} = 245 \text{ lb-ft}$$

Then, if you divide both sides of the equation by 100 lb, you have:

$$x = 2.45 \text{ ft}$$

This data would tell you that your friend's center of mass is 2.45 feet (2 ft $7/16$ inches) above the bottom of his feet, a distance that can be measured.

Make the actual measurements and find your friend's center of mass. Then ask your friend to raise his arms so that if he were standing, his hands would be well above his head. Repeat the experiment with your friend in this position. What happens to his center of mass?

Have your friend help you find your center of mass using this same experiment. How does your center of mass compare with his?

Having done the experiments in this book, you're aware of how forces affect the motion of objects and how they can cause work to be done. Now you can use what you've learned to better understand the motions and work you see being accomplished in your daily life.

Appendix

SCIENCE SUPPLY COMPANIES

Carolina Biological Supply Company
2700 York Road
Burlington, NC 27215-3398
(800) 334-5551
http://www.carolina.com

**Connecticut Valley Biological
    Supply Company**
82 Valley Road
P.O. Box 326
Southampton, MA 01073
(800) 628-7748
http://www.ctvalleybio.com

Delta Education
80 Northwest Boulevard
P.O. Box 3000
Nashua, NH 03061-3000
(800) 258-1302
http://www.delta-education.com

Educational Innovations, Inc.
362 Main Avenue
Norwalk, CT 06851
(888) 912-7474
http://www.teachersource.com

Fisher Science Education
4500 Turnberry Drive
Hanover Park, IL 60133
(800) 955-1177
http://www.fisheredu.com

Frey Scientific
80 Northwest Boulevard
Nashua, NH 03063
(800) 225-3739
http://www.freyscientific.com/

NASCO-Fort Atkinson
901 Janesville Avenue
P.O. Box 901
Fort Atkinson, WI 53538-0901
(800) 558-9595
http://www.nascofa.com/

NASCO-Modesto
4825 Stoddard Road
P.O. Box 3837
Modesto, CA 95352-3837
(800) 558-9595
http://www.eNasco.com

Sargent-Welch
P.O. Box 4130
Buffalo, NY 14217
(800) 727-4368
http://www.sargentwelch.com

Science Kit & Boreal Laboratories
777 East Park Drive
P.O. Box 5003
Tonawanda, NY 14151-5003
(800) 828-7777
http://sciencekit.com

Ward's Natural Science
P.O. Box 92912
Rochester, NY 14692-9012
(800) 962-2660
http://www.wardsci.com

Further Reading

Bochinski, Julianne Blair. *The Complete Workbook for Science Fair Projects*. Hoboken, N.J.: Wiley, 2005.

Bug, Amy. *Forces and Motion*. New York: Chelsea House, 2008.

Green, Dan. *Physics*. New York: Kingfisher, 2008.

Haduch, Bill. *Science Fair Success Secrets: How to Win Prizes, Have Fun, and Think Like a Scientist*. New York: Dutton Children's Books, 2002.

Hammond, Richard. *Can You Feel the Force?* New York: DK Pub., 2006.

Silverstein, Alvin, Virginia Silverstein, and Laura Silverstein Nunn. *Forces and Motion*. Minneapolis, Minn.: Twenty-First Century Books, 2009.

Vecchione, Glen. *Blue Ribbon Science Projects*. New York: Sterling Pub. Co., 2005.

Other books by Robert Gardner:

Gardner, Robert. *Physics Projects with a Light Box You Can Build*. Berkeley Heights, N.J.: Enslow Publishers, Inc., 2008.

Gardner, Robert, Madeline Goodstein, and Thomas R. Rybolt. *Ace Your Physical Science Project: Great Science Fair Ideas*. Berkeley Heights, N.J.: Enslow Publishers, Inc., 2010.

Gardner, Robert and Madeline Goodstein. *Ace Your Forces and Motion Science Project: Great Science Fair Ideas*. Berkeley Heights, N.J.: Enslow Publishers, Inc., 2010.

Internet Addresses

All Science Fair Projects
    <http://www.all-science-fair-projects.com/>

Exploratorium
    <http://www.exploratorium.edu/>

TryScience. "Experiments."
    <http://www.tryscience.org/experiments/experiments_home.html/>

Index